INTERESTING & INFLUENTIAL PEOPLE OF ORANGEBURG

INTERESTING & INFLUENTIAL

PEOPLE OF ORANGEBURG

GENE ATKINSON

THE History PRESS

Published by The History Press
Charleston, SC 29403
www.historypress.net

Front cover images: Water wheel, courtesy of E.J. Lackey. Portraits, *left to right*: Wallace C. Bethea, courtesy of Merle B. Cox; Marion B. Wilkinson, courtesy of Gerry Zimmerman; Mary W. Williams, courtesy of Mary W. Williams; George Cornelson, courtesy of the City of Orangeburg.

Back cover image: The first bale of cotton ginned in the 1925 season. *Courtesy of Katheryn Jeffords.*

First published 2010

Manufactured in the United States

ISBN 978.1.59629.735.7

Library of Congress Cataloging-in-Publication Data

Atkinson, Gene (William Gene)
Interesting and influential people of Orangeburg / Gene Atkinson.
p. cm.
Includes index.
ISBN 978-1-59629-735-7
1. Orangeburg County (S.C.)--Biography. 2. Orangeburg County (S.C.)--History, Local. I. Title.
F277.O5A85 2010
975.7'790099--dc22
2010015897

CONTENTS

Preface and Acknowledgements 7

Chapter 1. 1850–1900 9
Chapter 2. 1900–1950 31
Chapter 3. 1950–2010 95

Index 219
About the Author 223

PREFACE AND ACKNOWLEDGEMENTS

Over the years I have become increasingly more intrigued in Orangeburg's history. For many years I have collected numerous old pictures from Orangeburg's past. The reception I have received from producing two pictorial histories in 2002 and 2004 has been overwhelming.

Over the last several years, I have begun to realize that not much has been written about the people who have made Orangeburg tick. Thus, the idea for a compilation of local biographies began to take shape. After five years of collecting research on notable citizens, the basis for such a book began to mature. Unfortunately, there are far more interesting people to write about than could be contained within the confines of this book. So who knows if another volume may be lurking in the future should the reception of this book be favorable.

There are many people I would like to thank collectively for the wonderful cooperation I received in response to my requests for information on their family members to make this publication possible. For this I am truly appreciative.

Additionally, I would like to thank the volunteers at the Orangeburg County Historical Society for their assistance in helping me procure my research. The files so aptly collected there through the years by Orangeburg's premier archivist, Hugo Ackerman, were immeasurable. Also, the microfilm collection of *The Times and Democrat* at the county library has been extremely beneficial. Mrs. E. Louise from the Naudin-Dibble Heritage Foundation Archives in Columbia needs to be especially commended for her excellent research and assistance in providing informative African American history in Orangeburg for this book. Her thoroughness was unparalleled. Dean Livingston ably assisted with the proofreading as well as provided much guidance and insight throughout the process.

Sadly, one of the guiding lights in my career died the first week I began writing the narrative of this book. Mrs. Carrie Cope, my high school English teacher for three years, has had more impact on my career in writing than anyone. Her firm but gentle nurturing during those formative years has certainly helped make my publications possible.

It is my sincere wish that anyone reading this book can learn more about the people who helped make the progress of Orangeburg possible through the years. For instance, did you know that Clemson University's rich football program was begun by an Orangeburg native in 1896, or that a lady from Orangeburg told off General Sherman, or that a graduate from Orangeburg High School won the Nobel Prize for Medicine in 1998? It is all here in this book.

CHAPTER 1

1850–1900

Norman A. Bull (1821–1901)

N.A. Bull was a leader in Orangeburg's mercantile business in the 1800s, amassing quite a fortune. He was considered to be the wealthiest citizen in town at his death in 1901. Mr. Bull possessed a soul of honor, and his word was his bond.

Born in Harwinton, Connecticut, in 1821, he came to Orangeburg in 1842 and went into business with his older brother and later another Harwinton native, Warren Scoville. The firm was named Case, Bull & Co. but in 1857 was changed to Bull, Scoville & Co. Mr. Bull was a very adept businessman. Planters from miles around would trade with him. They paid their accounts in cotton for the preceding year and received goods for the next year on credit. Interest was paid in cotton. During the Civil War, any cotton Mr. Bull could get through the blockade to England fetched a high price. He was wise enough to leave the money paid for this in the Bank of England, which allowed him to accumulate a small fortune.

In 1865, the firm became known as Bull, Scoville & Pike but reverted to Bull and Scoville in 1876. From the Civil War on, it was located at the east corner of the town square on Russell Street where the S.H. Kress Co. was located in the middle of the twentieth century. By the time 1900 rolled around, Mr. Bull had built a handsome block of buildings all the way to Pitthan Alley, now Wall Street. These prestigious buildings became known as Bull Block.

In addition to its cotton brokerage business, the main store housed general merchandise from groceries and dry goods to agricultural implements

Courtesy City of Orangeburg.

and other farm supplies. The firm handled from four to six thousand bales of cotton annually. Additionally, Bull and Scoville became the first fire and life insurance agents in the county, representing several underwriters, including the Hartford Fire Insurance Company.

In the military regime after the Civil War, Mr. Bull was appointed "intendant" of Orangeburg, serving as the administrative leader in town. In 1868, he was unanimously elected mayor by both the white and African American populations and was successful in reinstating order out of chaos. He was reelected and served through 1871. During that time, he led Orangeburg to becoming an incorporated city in 1871.

Mr. Bull helped establish the Bank of Orangeburg after a recession diminished the previous banking industry here. He also established the Orangeburg Street Railway in 1888 and the cotton oil mill.

N.A. Bull built prestigious homes for his children on Russell Street, where a shopping center now exists between Centre and Lowman Streets. Quietly, he assisted many people less fortunate, as well as taking care of his servants' needs. He was a devout member of the First Presbyterian Church in town.

In 1852, he married Elizabeth B. Elliott, the daughter of prominent local physician Dr. Thomas A. Elliott. They had five children: Harriet Dotha, John Elliott, Norman Henry, Lizzie Austin and Ella Dudley. Mr. Bull died in 1901 after a long and distinguished business career in Orangeburg.

GEORGE H. CORNELSON (1842–1916)

George H. Cornelson is considered to be the one person who has had more impact on Orangeburg than anyone else over the last 150 years. Because of his influence, Orangeburg grew from a small village to a bustling city by the time of his death in 1916.

Courtesy City of Orangeburg.

Born in Ottersburg, Germany, in 1842, Mr. Cornelson came to New York City at age twenty-three. He worked there for a brief period before coming to Orangeburg. Using his modest savings, he opened a general merchandise store in town that prospered in spite of the postwar economy. With his sharp business skills, he expanded his store as well as began new enterprises, the largest of which was Orange Cotton Mills. This was the first cotton mill in the lower part of the state. Because of its resounding success, he was able to build a mill village for his employees, with housing as well as a church.

When Orangeburg needed to establish a water system in 1887, he built it himself and leased it to the city as it did not have the funds to do so itself. Mr. Cornelson also built the first telephone system in Orangeburg that ran from his place of business downtown to his home on Railroad Avenue (now Webber Boulevard). He also built the first ice plant in this part of the state.

Mr. Cornelson built an array of enterprises during his life in Orangeburg. Additionally, he helped some of his apprentices start businesses for themselves. His philanthropy was legendary, contributing in many ways to benefit Orangeburg. His generosity also helped individuals avoid bankruptcy when hard times appeared. He did all this without ostentation or publicity. He truly believed in making Orangeburg a better city in which to live.

As a faithful member of First Presbyterian Church in Orangeburg, he liberally provided funds for church causes. Mr. Cornelson also deeply contributed to Thornwell Orphanage and Presbyterian College.

In 1869, he married Miss Angie M. Holman, and they had four children: Reverend George Cornelson Jr., Emma C. Dantzler, Annie C. McLees and Professor Charles Arthur Cornelson.

If there was ever anyone who made the largest impact on the city of Orangeburg over the years, George Cornelson would have to be the one to fit that bill.

Samuel Dibble (1837–1913)

Samuel Dibble was an eminent lawyer, scholar, statesman, builder and educator. He was a man of broad vision and clearly had an impact on our economy as well as establishing an education system for Orangeburg.

Mr. Dibble was born in Charleston in 1837 to Philander Virgil and Frances Ann Dibble. His early education was in Charleston, and his college education was at the College of Charleston and Wofford College, where he graduated in 1856. After college, he taught at two Orangeburg academies and at Wofford's Preparatory Department. While in Spartanburg, he studied law and was admitted to the bar. He began his law practice in 1860 in Orangeburg. During the Civil War, he volunteered to serve with the Edisto Rifles.

After the war, he returned to Orangeburg and formed a partnership with James F. Izlar under the firm name of Izlar and Dibble. Profoundly versed in the law, his abilities were unparalleled, including arguing many notable causes. He was also editor of the *Orangeburg News*.

Mr. Dibble was elected to the South Carolina House of Representatives in 1876 and elected as one of the trustees of South Carolina College (now the University of South Carolina) in 1878. He was also chairman of the executive committee of the South Carolina Agricultural College and Mechanics Institute for colored students. Dibble also was appointed to the Board of Commissioners that formulated Orangeburg County into local school districts. In 1880, he was a delegate to the Democratic National Convention as well as being chosen as a presidential elector. In 1881, he was elected to the United States House of Representatives, in which body he served until 1891.

Courtesy Tony Emanuel.

In addition to his reputation as an able lawyer and leader, he was a very able businessman.

He was a founder and first president of the Edisto Savings Bank (later Edisto National Bank) and president of both the Bowman Land and Improvement Company and the Branchville and Bowman Railroad Company.

He was president of the Young America Steam Fire Engine Company as well as its chief. Mr. Dibble was Sunday school superintendent at St. Paul's Methodist Church for many years. He was considered to be the best-educated and most broadly informed man in the county. The large, spacious home he built on Russell Street was a downtown landmark for years (now the location of the vacant Winn-Dixie grocery store on Russell Street).

In 1864, he married Mary Christiana Louis, and they had four children: Frances Agnes Dibble Moss, Mary Henley Dibble Watson, Samuel Dibble and Louis Dibble. He died in 1913.

John H. Dukes (1834–1917)

John Henry Dukes was born in 1834 in Orangeburg to John W.H. and Martha B. Dukes. His early education was in Orangeburg. At age twenty, he left school to pursue a career in agriculture with his father. In 1862, Mr. Dukes enlisted in the Confederate army and was stationed as a sergeant on the South Carolina coast until 1864, when he was sent to Virginia. While there, he participated in several significant battles, including the Battle of Coal Harbor. When his unit returned to South Carolina, it helped defend Columbia during Sherman's march through the South. He was among the last soldiers to leave that city.

Courtesy Jimmy Rickenbacker.

In 1886, Mr. Dukes was elected to the South Carolina House of Representatives for the first of three terms. He also was active in Masonry. Religiously, he was a very active member of St. Paul's Methodist Episcopal Church.

John H. Dukes was the beloved Orangeburg County sheriff for sixteen years and was affectionately known as "Uncle John" by all.

He was married to the former Sophia Janette in 1857, and they had fourteen children: eleven boys and three girls. Mr. Dukes was the patriarch of a long line of successful heirs. Among these were a mayor of Orangeburg for ten years, a successful lawyer and the founder of one of Orangeburg's most prominent funeral homes.

JOHN WILLIAM HAZELWOOD DUKES (1858–1918)

J.W.H. Dukes was born in 1858 to John Henry and Sophia Dukes, the oldest of fourteen children. He was the mayor of Orangeburg from 1891 to 1901 and again from 1907 to 1911. During his progressive tenure as mayor, the first city waterworks was established, the first electric streetlights were installed and the first road was paved in the city.

Mr. Dukes was prominent in several business enterprises in town. He was the principal owner and operator of the Orangeburg street trolley system that operated from 1888 to 1908.

On a humanitarian note, he was lauded by a local minister who said that when a poor person died and the family was unable to hire a carriage for the funeral, Mr. Dukes would always send the finest carriage he owned.

Courtesy Jimmy Rickenbacker.

Mr. Dukes was a faithful member of St. Paul's Methodist Episcopal Church. He was also a member of the local lodge of the Knights of Pythias.

He married Lucia Bee Lowman, and they had six children: Walter W. Dukes, T. Earle Dukes, Mrs. L.E. Shecut, Mrs. J.G. Wannamaker Jr., Marguerite Dukes and Mrs. Robert S. McCants. He died in 1918 after being in failing health for several years.

Reverend Lewis Marion Dunton (1848–1936)

As the third president of Claflin University, Lewis Dunton served with honor and distinction. His organizational skills and fundraising capabilities propelled Claflin through hard times to where it experienced exceptional growth.

Reverend Lewis Dunton was born in 1848 in Martinsburg, New York. His educational experiences were at Cazenonia and Talley Seminaries, as well as at Syracuse University. He moved to South Carolina in 1873 upon medical advice that the southern climate might be beneficial for a lung condition that he was experiencing.

Reverend Dunton was ordained in 1874 and served churches in Greenville and Charleston. While at Centenary Church in Charleston, he was asked to help Claflin as a special agent with the responsibilities to replace the main building that had been destroyed by a recent fire. He traveled to the north to secure donations from churches and various organizations. Because of his success in doing so, he was named vice-president of Claflin as well as a professor of mental philosophy and logic. As a result of his outstanding abilities, he was named president of Claflin in 1884 and remained so for thirty-eight years until his retirement in 1922. He also was head of the A&M college until it separated from Claflin in 1896 to become the Colored, Normal, Agricultural and Mechanical College of South Carolina (now South Carolina State University). Reverend Dunton's wife, Mary, was equally energetic and, as an accomplished artist, led the art department. Together, their fundraising efforts proved to be very successful in acquiring funds to propel Claflin into a new century with many new buildings and exceptional academic progress.

Courtesy Claflin University Archives.

Dr. Dunton was an early advocate of physical fitness and established an athletic department that began to field teams in football, baseball and other sports. He even established a bicycle club to promote health and fitness.

During Dr. Dunton's tenure, the college's acreage increased from six to twenty-one acres, and many new buildings were constructed. He developed the academic program into one of the finest curricula available. Because of his outstanding leadership and fundraising abilities, he was honored with the title of president emeritus upon his retirement in 1922. In 1925, he was elected secretary treasurer of the Claflin College Endowment Fund. Reverend Dunton died in 1936 after a long and distinguished career at Claflin.

DR. THOMAS ARTERS ELLIOTT (1802–1884)

The large tombstone at the grave of Dr. Thomas Arters Elliott says it all: "T. Arters Elliott, Philanthropist, Gentleman, Christian…His Life an Inspiration to Posterity."

Dr. T.A. Elliott was born in Charleston to Christopher Robert and Elizabeth Elliott in 1802. He studied medicine under Dr. Samuel Dickson and graduated from the Medical College of Charleston (now MUSC). Dr. Elliott began his career practicing medicine in upper St. Matthews in 1827. About 1835, he moved to Orangeburg and resided in the large house formerly belonging to Dr. Thomas Glover. As time went on, his son-in-law, Dr. W.S. Dudley, joined him in practice. Later on, Dr. A.S. Salley and his son associated with him.

Courtesy Salley Johnson.

In 1836, Dr. and Mrs. Elliott were among the charter members of the First Presbyterian Church in Orangeburg. He was a leader there, serving as a senior ruling elder as well as being in charge of the State Bible Convention in 1861. He was a significant advocate of temperance and was a state leader in that cause.

Dr. Elliott was the fire chief for the first volunteer fire department established in Orangeburg in 1854, the Young America Company. In 1869, he formed a new volunteer fire department, and the members honored him by calling it the Elliott Hook and Ladder Company. Additionally, he led the efforts to establish underground fire cisterns for Orangeburg.

As a physician, he was widely known for his compassionate care, once traveling all the way to Aiken and back in a single day to see a patient.

In 1823, he married the former Harriet Badger. They had five children: Thomas, George, Jane Dudley, Elizabeth (Lizzie) Bull and Christopher. Both Thomas and George were killed in the Civil War.

Dr. Elliott was known as a kind, charitable, honest and noble man with an impeccable character. He left to Orangeburg a rich legacy with his service and exemplary life.

John Hammond Fordham (1854–1922)

John Hammond Fordham was born in 1854 in Charleston to Reverend Henry and Maria Fordham. His education was received at the Avery Institute there. He received further education studying under Reverend J.B. Seabrook and read law under E.B. Seabrook. In 1874, he was admitted to the South Carolina Bar and moved to Orangeburg, where he began the practice of criminal law.

Courtesy Louisa Robinson.

Being very active in the Republican Party, he was appointed to fill the unexpired term as coroner for Orangeburg County from 1874 to 1876. Choosing not to be a candidate for reelection, he became a statewide canvasser for the Republican Party, giving speeches in several counties across the state. In 1877, he was appointed postal clerk in the railway mail service, where he served until 1887. At that time, he resumed his law practice in Orangeburg.

In 1888, Mr. Fordham was selected as an alternate delegate to the Republican National

Convention held in Chicago. In 1889, he was appointed as the deputy collector for the Internal Revenue Service in South Carolina for the Second and later the First Division. Upon the onset of the term of President Grover Cleveland in 1893, Mr. Fordham retired and returned to his law practice here. After President McKinley came to office in 1897, he was appointed as South Carolina's deputy collector of the First Division again, a position he held until 1912, when he again returned to his law practice.

Mr. Fordham was an organizer of the Carolina Light Infantry of Charleston, the first all African American brigade in the South. He rose through the ranks and became judge advocate with the rank of major. Locally, "the Major," as he was called, helped organize two African American volunteer fire departments, the Comet and the Phoenix Hose Company. He was a devout member of Trinity Methodist Church in Orangeburg.

In 1875, Mr. Fordham married the former Louisa Smith, and they had nine children, three of whom died in infancy. He died in 1922 at the age of sixty-eight.

WILLIAM L. GLAZE (1854–1917)

"He gave justice to all, friendliness to many, and pity to the unfortunate." Thus reads the epitaph on the tombstone of William L. Glaze, one of Orangeburg's most public-spirited citizens.

William L. Glaze was born in Orangeburg County in 1854 and graduated from Wofford College in 1876. He became principal of Pine Grove Academy and afterward was an assistant to Professor Hugo Sheridan at the Sheridan Classical School in Orangeburg. In 1879, he began studying law under General James F. Izlar and was admitted to the bar in 1881, practicing with Mr. Izlar.

Mr. Glaze was chairman of the Orangeburg County Democratic Executive Committee for a number of years. About 1890, when the public schools were established here, he was on the first board of trustees for twenty years as well as being its first chairman. After twenty years, he resigned to accept an appointment as a member of the Winthrop College board of trustees.

As an able lawyer, he enjoyed an outstanding statewide reputation in the legal profession. In 1915, he was elected as a circuit judge for South Carolina but declined the position due to ill health.

Major Glaze was the city attorney for Orangeburg from 1885 until his death in 1917. He was also the attorney as well as a board member of the

Courtesy St. Paul's United Methodist Church.

Peoples National Bank. Mr. Glaze also served as president of the Orangeburg County Bar Association.

Major Glaze was a longtime member of the Masonic order and was its deputy grand master. He was a member of the Woodmen of the World and the Knights of Pythias.

Religiously, he was a devoted member of St. Paul's Methodist Church, where he served as a steward and was chief usher for many years. In 1892, he was appointed as chairman of the Building Committee to oversee the procurement of funds as well as the construction of the magnificent new church, which was completed in 1898.

Mr. Glaze married the former Emily Herbert, and they had six children: Herbert, Richard, William Jr., Minnie Herbert, Emily and Elizabeth. He died in 1917.

Judge Thomas Worth Glover (1796–1884)

Judge Thomas W. Glover lived an honored existence of public service to Orangeburg and the state of South Carolina. He was considered to be a shining example of decency.

Judge Glover was born in St. James Parish in Goose Creek, South Carolina, on Christmas Eve 1796. He and his family moved to Orangeburg in 1809. His pre-college training was at Mount Bethel, a celebrated preparatory school near Newberry. College followed at South Carolina College (now the University of South Carolina), where he graduated in 1817. Afterward, he studied law under the distinguished Chancellor Harper and was admitted to the bar in 1818.

At age twenty-six, Mr. Glover was elected to the South Carolina House of Representatives, where he served for sixteen years. In 1838, he was elected clerk of the House of Representatives, a position he held for fourteen years until his election as a circuit judge. In 1868, the Reconstruction government forced him to resign, whereupon he entered the practice of law with his second son, Mortimer Glover.

Mr. Glover built a large, imposing residence on Russell Street about 1828 that included much acreage all around. The main portion of this grand home still exists today, but its front has been changed to Whitman Street. The Episcopal Church of the Redeemer and the former Dukes-Harley Funeral Home are among the lots that comprised his large front yard. During Sherman's occupation of Orangeburg, the general made this home his headquarters. As Judge Glover was away during this time, his wife reminded General Sherman that she had known him as a young lieutenant at Fort Moultrie in the 1840s when she was a young lady in Charleston, and that "he conducted himself as a gentleman then, and she expected nothing less of him now." He gave orders for her house to be spared from destruction as a result.

Judge Glover married his first wife, Caroline Elizabeth Jamison, in 1824. She was the daughter of Dr. Van de Vastine Jamison, the first doctor in the Orangeburg District. One of her brothers was a founder of The Citadel, South Carolina's military college in Charleston. There were four sons and four daughters from this union. She died in 1856, and Judge Glover married Mrs. Louisa Wilson of Charleston in 1864. At age eighty-two, Judge Glover became the master in equity in Orangeburg, and he held that position until his death at age eighty-seven in 1884.

JUDGE JAMES F. IZLAR (1832–1912)

James F. Izlar held many positions of public trust, ably serving Orangeburg throughout his life. Soldier, lawyer, judge, congressman, state senator—Mr. Izlar was a true public servant.

Born in 1832 in the Fork section of Orangeburg County, his parents were William H. and Julia Izlar. He was educated at the Old Field Schools here and collegiately graduated from Emory College at Oxford, Georgia, in 1854, being first in his class. Mr. Izlar began the study of law in 1855 and was admitted to the bar in 1858. He began his law practice in Orangeburg but was interrupted by military service with the Edisto Rifles in the Confederate army during the Civil War.

After the war, it took him a year to regain possession of his law office to resume his practice. He partnered with Sam Dibble for eleven years until the latter was elected to the United States Congress. Mr. Izlar then practiced alone and later practiced with his son William L. Izlar, his brother Laurie T. Izlar and William L. Glaze. For sixteen years, he served on the state Democratic Party Executive Committee, being its chairman for ten years. He served three terms as a state senator before being elected as a circuit court judge. After that, he was elected to represent this area of the state in the United States House of Representatives.

Courtesy Orangeburg County Historical Society.

Businesswise, he was one of the organizers of the Bank of Orangeburg and was its president for about twenty years. Fraternally, he was a leader in Masonry, being the worshipful master for many years.

Mr. Izlar also served as a trustee of South Carolina College (now the University of South Carolina) as well as a member of Orangeburg's City Council.

In 1859, Mr. Izlar married Frances Lowell, and they had ten children. After Mrs. Izlar died in 1902, he married Marion Allston in 1906. Judge Izlar died in 1912.

For more than forty years, Judge Izlar was a prime mover in the business, social and political world in Orangeburg.

Theodore Kohn (1840–1902)

Theodore Kohn, growing up as a new immigrant in Orangeburg, became one of its leading citizens in the mercantile and banking industries. But perhaps his greatest contribution to our city came in the form of public education, as he was considered to be the "Father of the Orangeburg Graded Schools."

Born in Bavaria, Germany, near Munich in 1840, Theodore Kohn came to the United States in 1848 with his parents, Philip and Diane Kohn. At

Courtesy Bill Rollins.

age ten, his parents returned to Germany, so he went to live with his aunt and uncle, Mr. and Mrs. Deopold Louis, in Orangeburg. Mr. Louis was a prominent merchant, and young Theodore went to work with him learning the mercantile business.

When the Civil War broke out, he was one of the first to enlist in the Edisto Rifles and served in the Charleston area and in Virginia. He was severely wounded in the arm in Virginia and, after being hospitalized, returned to Orangeburg to recuperate. After regaining partial use of his arm, he rejoined his command in Virginia until the end of the Civil War.

In 1868, Theodore Kohn opened his own dry goods store in Orangeburg with a friend, a Mr. Ezekial. In 1869, his younger brother Henry joined him as a partner. The business ultimately became known as Theodore Kohn's Dry Goods Emporium. The great fire of 1875 destroyed his store as well as most of the downtown business district. The next year, he built a handsome new brick building that still stands today on Russell Street. Kohn's became Orangeburg's leading department store and offered quality and stylish fashions of the day.

Mr. Kohn was one of the original stockholders of the Edisto National Bank and was on its first board of directors. He was an alderman (city councilman) in 1883 and a member of the Young America Steam Engine Company volunteer fire department. He also was the assistant chief over all the volunteer fire departments for a while.

One of Theodore Kohn's greatest legacies to Orangeburg came in his commitment to education. He was on the original board of trustees for the Orangeburg schools that came into existence about 1890 and served until ill health forced his resignation shortly before his death in 1902.

Mr. Kohn was the treasurer of the Shibboleth Lodge of the local Masonic order for twenty-five years. He was also an active member of the Knights of Honor and recorder of the Orangeburg lodge since its inception.

In 1867, he married the former Rosa Waldheim from New York City, and they had seven children: August, Sol, David, Louis, Dina, Adeline and Bertha. Mr. Kohn died in 1902.

Deopold Louis (1816–1885)

Deopold Louis was a prominent businessman in Orangeburg in the 1800s. Mr. Louis was born in Bavaria, Germany, in 1815. He came to America as a penniless young man and settled in Orangeburg in the 1830s. At that time, Orangeburg was a small village with a scattering of houses and little promise of growth. Through his hard work and perseverance, he was able to start from scratch and become one of the leading merchants in Orangeburg. He was believed to be the first Jewish settler in town, being the pioneer of what later became a sizeable Jewish merchant class here.

Mr. Louis's character was impeccable, and he was considered to be extremely honest and upright in his business transactions. His philanthropy was indeed immeasurable. Despite the setback of being burned out in two or three fires, he rebounded from catastrophe each time. At the time of his retirement due to ill health two years before his death, he was the oldest merchant in Orangeburg. He was considered to be one of the wealthier citizens in Orangeburg. At the time of his death in 1885, he had lived in Orangeburg for nearly fifty years. Mr. Louis lived in a large home on Broughton Street at the corner of Amelia Street.

Mr. Louis married Ann Agnes Hall, and they had one daughter, Mary Christiana Louis Dibble.

Courtesy Tony Emanuel.

PROFESSOR STILES R. MELLICHAMP (1841–1922)

Stiles R. Mellichamp will be remembered as one of the leaders at the forefront of education in Orangeburg.

Professor Mellichamp was born on James Island near Charleston in 1841. His early education was obtained at the island school and Charleston High School. He went to the Charleston College (now the College of Charleston), but the entire class left several months before graduation to serve in the Confederate army. As a result, members of the class were given their diplomas in March 1861.

Mr. Mellichamp served as a member of the Moultrie Guards of the First Regiment of Rifles of Charleston and participated in the first Battle of Fort Sumter. After that, he was asked to serve as the teacher of the Marine School of Charleston, where he was devoted to the training of young sailors. After less than a year, he became part of the engineer corps for the Confederacy. He helped lay out batteries around Savannah and Macon, Georgia. Later, he went to Alabama to make topographical surveys for areas between Confederate and Union soldiers that were potential battlefields.

After the war, he returned to his love of teaching and served in Orangeburg, Elloree and Judyville before serving from 1870 to 1871 as a civil engineer to lay out the townships of Orangeburg County. In 1871, he returned to teaching in Orangeburg and opened his own private school.

Courtesy Orangeburg Consolidated School District 5.

In 1880, he was elected as school commissioner for Orangeburg County, serving a total of eight years. In 1878, he purchased the *Orangeburg Times*, a local newspaper that merged a few years later with *The Democrat* to become *The Times and Democrat*. He continued his editorial work there for seven more years, but his school duties compelled him to step down.

In 1890, the citizens of Orangeburg adopted the graded school system and consolidated all the private schools. Mr.

Mellichamp then became the principal of the female department. In 1891, he left to take charge of Furman University's preparatory school. In 1899, he returned to Orangeburg to teach at a local college, the Orangeburg Collegiate Institute.

At age eighty in 1921, Mr. Mellichamp was the honored guest at a reunion reception and banquet with his former pupils. Several hundred of his former students came to honor their venerable teacher. It was announced that night that the Sellers Avenue Graded School would now be called Mellichamp School, a significant honor for someone who had provided the educational foundation for practically everyone in Orangeburg.

In 1866, Mr. Mellichamp married Miss Sarah Miller, and they had three daughters: Mrs. Peter Brunson, Mrs. A.C. Ligon and Mrs. Edith Andrews. Professor Mellichamp died in 1922 after a long and distinguished career in the education of our young people in Orangeburg.

Thomas E. Miller (1849–1938)

Thomas E. Miller was considered to be one of the founders of South Carolina State University, as well as its first president from 1896 to 1911.

Born in St. Luke's Parish in Beaufort County, he was raised as a free person of color by Richard Miller and Mary Ferrebee. In a late life interview, Thomas Miller said that his father was a wealthy white man and his mother was the mulatto daughter of Judge Thomas Heyward Jr., a signer of the Declaration of Independence. He received his education in Charleston, South Carolina, and Hudson, New York. In 1872, he graduated from Lincoln University in Pennsylvania and in 1876 from law school at State University in Charleston. Mr. Miller served in the South Carolina House of Representatives from 1874 to 1880 and again from 1894 to 1896. He also served a term in the South Carolina Senate as well as the United States Congress from 1890 to 1892. As a member of the state constitutional convention in 1895–96, he prevailed in the establishment of a separate agricultural and mechanical college for African Americans. Previously, this had been part of Claflin University. Thus, the Colored Normal, Industrial, Agricultural, and Mechanical College of South Carolina (now South Carolina State University) was formed as a separate and state-supported college. It was only natural that Thomas Miller was chosen as its first president.

President Miller worked tirelessly and oversaw tremendous growth of the physical plant as well as the academic program. Unfortunately, he was forced

Courtesy E. Louise, Naudin-Dibble Heritage Foundation Collection.

to resign in 1911 after his political adversary became governor. Thomas Miller has been credited with being the one person most responsible for the creation and early success of South Carolina State University.

Mr. Miller was also one of the founders of St. Luke's Presbyterian Church in Orangeburg as well as serving as its pastor.

He married the former Anna Marie Hume from Charleston, and they had nine children. Mr. Miller died in 1938. The epitaph on his tombstone read, "I served God and all the people, loving the white man not less, but the Negro needed me most."

HARPIN RIGGS (1817–1893)

As an expert machinist, Harpin Riggs established shops that manufactured farm implements, carts, wagons, buggies and carriages. He also operated a cotton gin and a gristmill, not to mention being a contractor, an undertaker and Orangeburg's sheriff.

Harpin Riggs was born in 1817 in Harwinton, Connecticut. At the age of nineteen, he moved to Orangeburg to join his older brother, Merritt. His brother built a large eight-room residence on Broughton Street at the corner of Russell Street. Harpin bought this home from his brother in the 1840s and added eight more rooms.

Mr. Riggs established several businesses through the years. Among these were machine shops to repair and manufacture buggies, carriages, wagons, farm implements and even a hearse for his role as an undertaker. Mr. Riggs also had a wheelwright shop and a blacksmith shop. He also operated a cotton gin, the largest gristmill in town and a large farm. As a contractor, he built the Presbyterian and Methodist churches. He was also a founder of the first local volunteer fire department. Many young people boarded in his large home while serving as apprentices in his shops, as did several seminary students.

Mr. Riggs owned almost all the land on the west side of Broughton Street from Russell Street to beyond the Atlantic Coast Line Railroad. On his plantation near the railroad, he butchered hogs each winter and always remembered the needy during butchering time. Mr. Riggs had many setbacks in life but bounced back with tremendous energy and perseverance each time. He was burned out three times in five years, had his right hand cut off in a cotton gin accident in 1876 and lost his left hand at his planing mill in 1884. Undaunted, he had a pair of hooks made and could open doors, feed himself with an attachment and drive a carriage, as well as hold the reins when riding a horse. Despite his challenges, Mr. Riggs had more energy and courage than anyone around.

Mr. Riggs first married a Miss Gowan. After her death, he married Chivalette Rowe, and after her death he married Emma Gowan Rickenbaker, who was a sister of his first wife. He had six children: Henry Riggs, Mrs. A.L. Dukes, Jessie R. Bell, Walter Riggs, Mary Riggs and Arthur Riggs. His son Walter, as a professor at Clemson College, established and coached the first football team. He later served as Clemson's president from 1909 to 1924.

Dr. Alexander S. Salley (1818–1895)

Dr. Alexander S. Salley was a renowned physician in his day. He lived a life of honor and respect in Orangeburg County.

Dr. Salley was born in the Orangeburg area in 1818 to George Elmore and Margaret J. Salley. As was customary in his day, he studied under a physician even before going to medical school. Upon his graduation from the South Carolina Medical College in Charleston in 1843, he practiced medicine

Courtesy Salley Johnson.

in the "Fork" section of Orangeburg County. Later, he came back to Orangeburg to enter into a partnership with his preceptor, Dr. Thomas A. Elliott. In that day, doctors had to travel by horse and buggy on poorly maintained roads to do house calls on their patients.

When the Civil War broke out, Dr. Salley was the surgeon of his regiment and served on the South Carolina coast and in Virginia. After the war he was nominated, without his knowledge, to the South Carolina legislature and graciously served from 1866 to 1868.

Dr. Salley was considered to be one of the most knowledgeable and highly respected physicians. Later in life, he was joined in his medical practice by his son.

Dr. Alexander Salley married Julia E. Murrowe in 1845. By a peculiarity of fate, they were both born in the same house seven years apart. His grandparents occupied the house at his birth, and her parents lived there when she was born. They had nine children: Alexander McQueen Salley, Dr. Michael G. Salley, Caroline A. Salley, Edward L. Salley, Jacob S. Salley, Julian A. Salley, David J. Salley, Mary J. Salley and William W. Salley.

Dr. Salley was considered to be a man of high noble virtues. As a person of sterling qualities, he was held in high esteem by all in town.

PROFESSOR HUGO G. SHERIDAN (1833–1899)

Hugo Grotius Sheridan was a legend in the educational field in Orangeburg in the late 1800s. Before the days of public education, his Sheridan Classical School provided educational opportunities to many young men and women in Orangeburg.

Courtesy Orangeburg Consolidated School District 5.

Hugo Sheridan was born in Colleton County in 1833. His father was a wealthy planter as well as a renowned physician. His preparation for college was at the old Cokesbury School. In 1857, he graduated from South Carolina College, now known as the University of South Carolina. Afterward, he studied law and was admitted to the bar but was interrupted by the oncoming of the Civil War. Mr. Sheridan entered the Confederate army as a captain of a voluntary company. When his company's enlistment ended, he volunteered again and served in the ordnance department.

After the Civil War, Mr. Sheridan decided to devote his life to the noble profession of teaching. His first teaching endeavor was at Haigler's Academy in Cameron. In 1877, he established the Sheridan Classical School in the old fair building on Amelia Street in Orangeburg. It enjoyed a splendid reputation as a college preparatory school, and students came from all over the lower part of South Carolina to study there. Many had to be boarded at the homes of teachers and local citizens. At its peak there were over one hundred students and a faculty of three. Public schools came into being shortly after 1890, and Professor Sheridan became the principal of the boys' department. After a few years there he went to Bamberg to be headmaster of the Carlisle Fitting School.

Mr. Sheridan served in the South Carolina House of Representatives before and after the Civil War. In addition to his school duties, he was the editor of the *Orangeburg Times* and, later, a joint owner of the *Edisto Clarion*, which became *The Orangeburg Democrat*. He sold his interest to devote more time to the educational demands of his school.

At St. Paul's Methodist Church, he was the longtime Sunday school superintendent.

He died in 1899 after a distinguished career guiding the educational pursuits of many of Orangeburg's young men and women. A few years later, the school system named the Sheridan School after him for his many contributions to education.

DR. JACOB G. WANNAMAKER (1852–1919)

Courtesy Salley Johnson.

Dr. J.G. Wannamaker established a large pharmaceutical company in Orangeburg in the 1800s.

Dr. Wannamaker was born near Orangeburg in 1852. He spent most of his life in Orangeburg. His education was obtained at South Carolina College, now the University of South Carolina, and the South Carolina Medical College, now the Medical University of South Carolina in Charleston.

After medical school, he returned to Orangeburg and established a pharmaceutical concern in 1875. With his abilities as a wise planner and diligent business methods, the J.G. Wannamaker Manufacturing Co. became one of the largest drug concerns in the area. From 1877 to 1890, he and his brother-in-law operated the Wannamaker-Murray Wholesale Drug Company. However, he sold his interest in 1890 and returned to his original company, where he remained until his death.

Dr. Wannamaker was chairman of Orangeburg's city board of commissioners, which oversaw the operations of the city water and light plant. He was also an organizer and president of the Bank of Orangeburg.

Fraternally, Dr. Wannamaker was a member of the Masonic order and the Knights of Pythias. He was an active member at St. Paul's Methodist Church.

Dr. Wannamaker and his wife, Carrie, had five children: Goldie W. Holman, Carrie W. Dew, Jacob G. Wannamaker Jr., Lewis C. Wannamaker and Will J. Wannamaker. He died in 1919.

CHAPTER 2

1900–1950

JAMES M. ALBERGOTTI (1885–1965)

"Mr. Jim" Albergotti was a man of deep integrity in the Orangeburg area. His word was his bond, and he was always considered to be truthful and honest above board.

Born in 1885 in Orangeburg to John Schmidt Albergotti and Sarah Amelia Moss Albergotti, he graduated from Orangeburg High School in 1900, a class of just six boys and eight girls. He attended Wofford College but returned home to enter the cotton business, working for Mr. W.S. Lining at a salary of fifteen dollars a month. When he received his first paycheck, it was written for twenty-five dollars, so he approached his boss to report this mistake. Mr. Lining replied that Jim had done his work so well that he had given him an immediate raise. After a year or so, Mr. Albergotti decided to go into business for himself. He had a unique arrangement with the president of Edisto National Bank where he would borrow enough money in the morning to buy a bale of cotton, sell it and then repay his loan in the afternoon. Soon his credit rating was raised to five bales and ultimately three hundred bales after proving his worthiness. Eventually, he became a member of the Edisto National Bank's board of directors.

His proudest moment came in 1922 when he and his wife, the former St. Claire Brown, donated about $5,000 to establish a playground system in Orangeburg. Mrs. Albergotti then helped guide and direct the Playground Commission for twenty-five years. They are credited with establishing the first playground system in the United States. The original location was

Courtesy James M. Albergotti III.

in what is now the rose garden in Edisto Memorial Gardens. In 1950, it was relocated to the corner of Riverside and Seaboard Streets. A plaque there now commemorates the Albergottis for their kind generosity through the years.

Besides being successful in the cotton business, "Mr. Jim," as he was known, bought the A.C. Watson Insurance Agency in 1930 and operated that until he sold it in 1952 to Orangeburg Realty.

An avid member of St. Paul's Methodist Church, "Mr. Jim" read at least a chapter of the Bible every day.

Civically, Mr. Albergotti was a member of the Rotary Club, being a past president. Additionally, he was a Mason, a Knights Templar and a member of the Knights of Pythias, the Odd Fellows and the Elks.

He and Mrs. Albergotti were the parents of three children: Dr. J.M. Albergotti Jr., Mrs. Amelia Speth and Mrs. John W. Brantley. Mr. Albergotti died in 1965.

W. EUGENE ATKINSON (1882–1973)

W. Eugene Atkinson was born in Sumter County in 1882 and grew up on his father's farm there. He finished his education in Orangeburg and started his career here as a bookkeeper.

As time went on, he became very successful with myriad business interests in Orangeburg. Among these were farming, being a cotton broker, establishing the Atkinson Furniture Co. in 1911 and serving as president of Planter's National Bank as well as president of Bankers National Life Insurance. Planters National Bank was established in 1908, and in 1920 its resources were in excess of $1 million. He merged Bankers Life with Palmetto State Life in Columbia and became its president too. He was also very active in the real estate business.

Courtesy Gene Atkinson.

Civically, Mr. Atkinson was a driving force promoting the well-being of Orangeburg. He served as president of the Chamber of Commerce in both 1916 and 1937. In 1921, Mr. Atkinson was a founding charter member of the Rotary Club and served as its first president. Active in Masonry, he was a past master of the Shibboleth Lodge. He was a former high priest of the Royal Arch, a past eminent commander of the Knights Templar, a Shriner, a past chancellor of the Knights of Pythias and a member of the Benevolent and Protective Order of the Elks.

One of his most significant contributions to Orangeburg was in the area of healthcare. When Orangeburg's first hospital, a private one that was established in 1919, began to have financial woes in the early 1930s, its ownership was transferred to the counties of Orangeburg, Bamberg and Calhoun. Because of his business prowess, Mr. Atkinson was chosen as chairman of a newly created Board of Trustees to restore financial confidence as well as upgrade the facilities. It was determined that an entirely new physical plant was needed, and the new hospital was built in 1937 on Carolina Avenue. Atkinson was credited with being the preeminent force behind the creation of this state-of-the-art facility for the Orangeburg area.

Being a religious-minded person, W. Eugene Atkinson was a devout member of St. Paul's Methodist Church, where he served on the Administrative Board for many years, as well as being its chairman. He was also the statewide treasurer for the South Carolina Methodist Conference.

Mr. Atkinson married the former Agnes Holman in 1907, and they had three sons: E. Wilkes Atkinson, David H. Atkinson and William B. Atkinson. He died at age ninety-one in 1973.

LEONARD BENNETT (1869–1952)

Leonard Bennett was a pioneer of technology in Orangeburg. He established the first gun repair shop, the first bicycle shop and the first automobile dealership. He also was the first automobile owner here in 1904.

Born in England in 1869, his family moved to Orangeburg when he was seven years old, living on the Belleville Road about four miles from town. At age twenty-three, Leonard decided that he was not cut out for farming and came to town to open up Orangeburg's first gun repair shop at the corner of Russell and Church Streets next to the town square. Later, when bicycles came in style, people would bring their wheels for him to repair, thus developing what became Orangeburg's first bicycle repair shop.

Music was quite a love of Mr. Bennett. As a young man, he either walked or rode a mule or horse to town for orchestra practices. He was quite an accomplished violinist and played for Dr. Laurence Wolfe's orchestra and Henry Kohn's philharmonic orchestra, as well as being the solo cornetist for the Orangeburg Military Band. This band gave weekly outdoor concerts in the bandstand at the courthouse grounds on the square.

In 1903, he married Miss Addie Owen, daughter of B.B. Owen, who owned the largest carriage and wagon repair shop in the county. She was taking cornet lessons from him when the romance began to blossom. While on their honeymoon in Asheville, she had her first ride in a new-fangled invention called an automobile. Mr. Bennett paid three dollars an hour for them to ride in a White Steamer. The bug must have bitten, as he bought his first car in 1904, a used Oldsmobile in Savannah, and then drove it back to Orangeburg. It had no roof, no doors and no steering wheel and just a lever to steer it. Dusters and goggles were a must in those days due to all the dust and mud on the dirt roads. For the next two years, he was the sole automobile owner in Orangeburg.

Courtesy Michael Salley.

Later, his gun and bicycle shop spread out to become Orangeburg's first automobile dealership and parts store. It was located on lower Russell Street where Dickson's Shoe Shop is now.

Mr. Bennett became a trustee of Queen's College in Charlotte. He and his wife were the parents of three daughters, all college educated: Louise, Ethel and Bess. He died in 1952.

Joseph A. Berry (1876–1956)

Joseph A. Berry will be remembered as one of the most eloquent speakers of his day in a long career that spanned over fifty years as a member of the bar.

Born in 1876 in Branchville, his mother died when he was only eight years old, and his father died when he was twelve. As a result, he was without parental attention and was not even able to go to school further, having to work instead.

Because of his abilities, he came to the law firm of Glaze and Herbert in Orangeburg in 1897 to read law and was admitted to the bar by the South Carolina Supreme Court in May 1898. Shortly thereafter, he enlisted with the Edisto Rifles to serve in the Spanish-American War, with part of that enlistment in Cuba. Afterward, he was a member of the South Carolina Guard for many years, ultimately becoming a major.

Courtesy Nancy Berry.

In 1900, Mr. Berry associated with William C. Wolfe in the practice of law under the firm name of Wolfe and Berry. He served as secretary and treasurer of the Orangeburg County Democratic Executive Committee from 1904 to 1918 as well as being the first vice-president of the State Bar Association. In 1914, he was elected to the South Carolina

House of Representatives, serving as speaker pro tem from 1917 to 1920. While in the House, he was considered to be one of its most eloquent speakers. Mr. Berry was chairman of the powerful Judiciary Committee as well as the Rules Committee. He made convincing speeches to establish a state highway commission when cars began to be prevalent, a state budget law, the state tax commission, a major expansion of The Citadel and a bill to repeal laws prohibiting Greek fraternities in state-supported colleges. In 1920, Joe Berry was unsuccessful in seeking the Senate seat for Orangeburg County.

Although his education was limited, he was an enthusiastic supporter of the Dixie Library, an Orangeburg volunteer library, before the advent of a public library system. This library even operated out of a room in his home for a while. During World War I, he was one of the most sought-after patriotic speakers in the county while also serving as county chairman of the War Saving Stamp (Bond) campaign.

Mr. Berry was a loyal member of St. Paul's Methodist Church in Orangeburg, a past chancellor of the Knights of Pythias, a past exalted ruler of the Elks and a Mason.

For many years, he and Mrs. Berry used their large downtown antebellum home as the Berry Tourist Home, providing rooms for out-of-town travelers. It was located on Russell Street where the popular local fast-food restaurant the Dairy O conducts business now.

In 1900, Joe Berry married Fannie Pike, and they had three children: James Brewton, Richard Pike and Joseph Andrew. In 1948, Mr. Berry was the honoree of a large testimonial dinner on his fiftieth anniversary of being a member of the bar. He died in 1956.

WALLACE C. BETHEA (1894–1982)

Wallace Carlisle Bethea without a doubt has been one of the most influential persons involving economic development in Orangeburg through the years.

Born near Darlington in 1894, Mr. Bethea graduated from Wofford College and Duke University in 1914. His first job afterward was with Spartanburg Grain and Mill Company. During World War I, he served in the U.S. Army in both France and Germany.

In 1919, Mr. Bethea began his legendary business career here in Orangeburg as the manager of his father-in-law's concern, the J.W. Smoak Hardware Co., a position he held until his retirement at age eighty-seven in 1981.

Courtesy Merle Cox.

In 1925, Mr. Bethea began a tenure of forty-five years serving on the Board of Trustees of South Carolina State University, a historic black college. He was also secretary of the board from 1925 to 1966. Unprecedented growth occurred at SC State during his service. In 1955, the newest and largest dormitory being constructed was named Bethea Hall in his honor. His wise business acumen helped SC State achieve financial stability during his tenure.

Wallace Bethea helped organize and establish First National Bank in Orangeburg in 1933 on the heels of the Depression. He served as its president and chairman, guiding its success for over forty years.

Mr. Bethea also served on the local Orangeburg school board for twelve years as well as being its chairman. As early as 1936, he had stressed that African American school facilities were inadequate and their teachers' salaries were too low. His efforts secured the establishment of the first African American public high school in Orangeburg, known as Wilkinson High, in 1937, as well as sought equitable salaries for teachers.

For the first half of the twentieth century, agriculture drove the economy in Orangeburg. In the 1950s, wise business leaders like Mr. Bethea realized that the agricultural business was beginning to dwindle and saw the need to actively seek manufacturing industries to sustain our economy. Thus, in 1956, the Orangeburg County Planning and Development Commission was formed, and of course Wallace Bethea was its chairman. It is said that when one prospective industry decided to locate in another city, Mr. Bethea inquired as to the reason. He was told that the company really preferred to come to Orangeburg but that it would cost $50,000 more in site preparation to do so. Mr. Bethea then wrote a personal check to the company for the $50,000 to cover that expense, and the industry came to Orangeburg.

Mr. Bethea's civic activities include being a past president of the Chamber of Commerce, a founder and second president of the Rotary Club of

Orangeburg, chairman of the Board of Stewards at St. Paul's Methodist Church, charter member of the Country Club of Orangeburg in 1922, a founder of the South Carolina Milk Producers Association and president of the Coastal Milk Producers Association. In 1959, he was selected as the Citizen of the Year in Orangeburg. Fraternally, he was a Mason and a member of the Elks, the American Legion and the VFW.

In 1917, he married Merle Smoak, the daughter of prominent Orangeburg businessman J.W. Smoak. They had three daughters: Lillian B. Rembert, Lynda B. Borden and Merle B. Cox.

Economically, Wallace Bethea made a significant imprint on Orangeburg over the years. The impact of his effort is truly immeasurable. He died at age eighty-eight in 1982.

JUDGE ILDERTON WESLEY BOWMAN (1857–1924)

Judge I.W. Bowman was born in 1857 near the old Cattle Creek Campground outside of Rowesville, South Carolina, to Dr. Orrin N. Bowman and Isabella Limehouse Bowman. He grew up on the family farm and attended country schools. At age seventeen, he attended Mount Zion Institute as preparation to enter Wofford College, where he graduated in 1879.

Courtesy Reddick Bowman.

Shortly after college graduation, he began reading law in the office of Sam Dibble while also teaching school in Rowesville from 1879 to 1880. After being admitted to the bar in December 1882, his reputation as a skillful lawyer steadily grew through the years. He was the attorney for Home Building and Loan Association, the largest institution of its kind in Orangeburg, as well as being its secretary for many years.

From 1894 to 1896, he served as a member of the South Carolina House of Representatives and was chosen to be a member of the Constitutional Convention in 1895 to draft a new state constitution. He was an unswerving advocate for the provision that prohibited divorce. In 1907, Mr. Bowman was elected to City Council in Orangeburg and in 1913 was elected by the legislature to be the judge for the First Judicial Circuit in South Carolina. He served in this capacity with distinction until his sudden death in 1924.

Judge Bowman was very active at St. Paul's Methodist Church, being its assistant Sunday school superintendent. He was also his church's delegate on four occasions to the Annual Conference of the South Carolina Methodist Church.

In 1883, he married the former Mary Ellen Crum from Denmark, South Carolina, and they had nine children. His spacious former home on the corner of Amelia and Lowman Streets was recently restored by the current owners.

Mayor James M. Brailsford (1882–1959)

James Moncrief Brailsford was born in Clarendon County in 1882 to John Moncrief and Camilla Brock Brailsford. His early education was at Panola School. He continued his education in Orangeburg at the Orangeburg Collegiate Institute, graduating at age sixteen. Mr. Brailsford remained there for an additional two years as commandant. Afterward, he taught school for a year at West Springs before attending the University of South Carolina School of Law. While there, he played on USC's football team, but because of his heavy study load he was only able to play at home games.

Courtesy City of Orangeburg.

After law school, he came to Orangeburg and set up a law office on Law Range, now Church Street, across from the courthouse. In 1907, he married Bessie Bates, a Winthrop graduate and the first paralegal secretary in Orangeburg, who incidentally worked for another law firm. As time went on, he began to purchase parcels of land and sharecrop them.

In 1932, he began his public service career for Orangeburg by being a member of City Council for two terms, as well as being mayor pro tem. This was followed by his being elected mayor from 1940 to 1944. While on City Council, he worked closely with the city-owned Orangeburg Water and Light Department to make sure citizens could receive affordable electricity and water, which, incidentally, had the lowest rates in the state.

During World War II, he headed up the Federal Land Bank for Orangeburg, where he was able to help save many farms and homes from bankruptcy. While these landowners were away at war, he protected their interests.

In 1919, when Orangeburg did not have a hospital, he was contacted by Dr. Charles Mobley from Rock Hill to help find a suitable location for him to establish Orangeburg's first hospital. They rode around town almost all day but came up empty-handed. As a last resort, he took Dr. Mobley to see one of the old buildings from the defunct Orangeburg Collegiate Institute that he had purchased and just finished remodeling into an apartment building. Dr. Mobley immediately jumped at this building, saying it was the only place in town he could use. Mr. Jim then agreed to sell him the building so that Orangeburg could have its first hospital.

In 1921, he helped purchase the land for Orangeburg's first country club. He also was one of the founders of the Rotary Club here in 1921.

He and Mrs. Brailsford had five children: Judge James M. Brailsford Jr., John Francis Brailsford, Camilla B. Knotts Williams, Elizabeth Brailsford and Sallie B. Kiser. He died in 1959.

THOMAS F. BRANTLEY (1867–1931)

Thomas F. Brantley was one of the most eloquent speakers and debaters in his era in law and politics.

Mr. Brantley was born and grew up on a farm about seven miles outside of Orangeburg in 1867. Because farming consumed a significant portion of his time, he was able to go to school only in the winter. He saved his money and also borrowed to send himself to Bingham Military School in North Carolina for two years. After returning to Orangeburg, he ran a small farm and taught school for two years before entering South Carolina College (now USC) in Columbia, where he graduated in 1892. During this time, he was able to secure a night teaching job in one of the mill villages to support his education. While at college, he had the reputation of being one of the most convincing and eloquent debaters, winning the coveted Debater's Medal his senior year.

After college, Mr. Brantley became a division chief at the United States Department of the Treasury in Washington, D.C., under the Cleveland administration. At night, he attended law lectures at Georgetown University, from which he graduated in 1894. Because of his powerful oratory, he was recruited by the Democratic Party to assist William Jennings Bryan in his presidential campaign in 1896. His campaign speeches received national attention, but unfortunately his superior at the Treasury Department was of the opposite political persuasion and dismissed him from his job. Mr. Brantley returned to Orangeburg after the election to establish his local law practice. In 1898 and 1900, he was elected to the South Carolina House of Representatives and in 1902 was elected to the state senate.

Courtesy Yates Snowden, History of South Carolina.

When the national presidential campaign of 1908 came about, he, as a delegate to the Democratic National Convention, again enthusiastically supported his good friend William Jennings Bryan, who became the nominee. Brantley spoke all over the United States, making his usual eloquent speeches on behalf of Mr. Bryan. Unfortunately, Mr. Bryan did not win this time either.

In 1926, Mr. Brantley was again elected to South Carolina's House of Representatives. Locally, he was a member of the First Baptist Church, a Mason, a past exalted ruler of the Elks and a past chancellor commander of the Knights of Pythias.

He married the former Estelle Fairey in 1905, and they had four children: Mary Ellison Brantley, Henrietta Estelle Brantley, Thomas F. Brantley Jr. and John W. Brantley. Mr. Brantley died in 1931.

ALTON E. BYTHEWOOD (1876–1937)

Alton E. Bythewood established the first African American funeral home in Orangeburg in 1907.

Mr. Bythewood was born in 1876 in Beaufort to Daniel and Catherine Bythewood. He attended Claflin University for his preparatory and college education. In 1907, he and his partner established the Bythewood and Ballard Funeral Home at the corner of Amelia and Middleton Streets. In the early years, the building burned down and had to be rebuilt. By 1919, Mr. Bythewood had become the sole owner and renamed it the Bythewood Funeral Home. In 1923, he enlarged the building significantly. At one time, this business was considered to be one of the largest African American funeral services in South Carolina. Today, this establishment is still providing mortuary services under the same name; however, the Bythewood family no longer operates it.

Mr. Bythewood also served as treasurer and manager of the Orangeburg Cemetery Association for many years. He was also state president of the Colored Embalmers Association and was one of its mainstays from the time that it was organized. Mr. Bythewood was also elected vice-president of the National Colored Embalmers Association for the whole nation in 1929.

Courtesy City of Orangeburg.

In 1906, he married the former Felicia A. Sasportas, daughter of prominent citizens Thaddeus K. and Mary Sasportas. They had three children: Dr. Alton E. Bythewood Jr., Thaddeus K. Bythewood and Mary Lou B. Lynch. He died in 1937.

Mr. Bythewood was well known as a pioneer and leader in the funeral home industry. Today, the Bythewood Funeral Home is celebrating over one hundred years of mortuary services to the Orangeburg community.

JAMES CARLISLE "CUTIE" CAUTHEN (1895–1984)

J.C. Cauthen was born in 1895 to a Methodist minister, Reverend Andrew J. Cauthen, and his wife, Mattie A. Cauthen. Because his father's profession encompassed frequent moves, Mr. Cauthen grew up in Methodist parsonages all across South Carolina.

"Cutie" Cauthen graduated from Wofford College in 1916 with both bachelor's and master's degrees. He then became employed by Southern Bell Telephone Co. in Atlanta, Georgia, as an engineer. When the United States entered World War I, he enlisted and became a radio officer and pilot, ultimately serving in France and Germany.

Upon Mr. Cauthen's return from the war, he and one of his brothers entered the automobile business. As a child, he had worked for automobile agencies as a mechanic's helper as well as a driver. In those days, it was a common practice that after the sale of an automobile, the dealer would provide a young man for a week or so to chauffer the new owner as well as to instruct him on how to drive this new purchase. As a result, Mr. Cauthen had become quite knowledgeable with makes of cars such as Firestone-Columbus, Metz, Cole, Regal, Reo, Maxwell and Studebaker—all now nonexistent.

Courtesy The Times and Democrat.

After a few years in the automobile industry, the brothers switched to the electrical contracting business due to a downturn in the economy due to the boll weevil infestation that destroyed the principal crop of the area: cotton.

In 1926, politics beckoned, and Mr. Cauthen was elected county auditor, a position he held for twenty years. As time went on, he developed an interesting and remunerative sideline repairing and servicing adding machines, typewriters, etc. at his home workshop. It was the only such business between Columbia and Charleston. During World War II, the Hawthorne School of

Aeronautics kept him quite busy with its office equipment. It seems that the dust created by all the airplane propellers on the dirt airfield created havoc with the office machines.

In 1946, Mr. Cauthen became Orangeburg's postmaster, serving until his retirement in 1965. He was a charter member and a past president of the Lions Club here, as well as had perfect attendance at meetings for over twenty-five years. Additionally, he was the treasurer for the Orangeburg County chapter of the American Red Cross for many years.

Mr. Cauthen married the former Nell Barton in 1920, and they had two children: Nell Cauthen Bundrick and Jimmie Cauthen. Mrs. Cauthen died in 1935, and he married the former Mildred Ellison in 1940, when she was serving in Orangeburg as a public health nurse.

JAMES FISHER CLECKLEY (1879–1964)

James Fisher Cleckley was a respected farmer, road construction contractor, manufacturer and banker. He was born on the family farm near Cope, South Carolina, in 1879 to Dr. James M. Cleckley and Rebecca Jennings Cleckley.

His education included attending Carlisle Fitting School in Bamberg and later Wofford College along with his twin brother. Because of family finances after the death of his father, he returned home to the family farm in 1897 while his twin brother continued at college to become a doctor. Mr. Cleckley operated the family farm in Cope until the late 1940s.

Courtesy The Times and Democrat.

In the 1920s, Mr. Cleckley entered the road construction business, using mules to drag pans and pull graders. An exceptionally large and strong mule was needed for this purpose, so he purchased a special jackass stud and mated him to large mares on his farm to produce these "Clydesdales" of mules. Eventually, power road grading machines replaced these mules. His company, which ultimately became the J.F. Cleckley Company, was one of the first road contractors to be licensed by the State of South Carolina.

On his farm, he experimented with a hand-operated machine to make concrete blocks, which he used to construct several farm buildings. This led him to establish the Farmers' Concrete Products Co. in the 1940s with Hinchie A. McGee. This firm manufactured concrete blocks and other concrete products. Additionally, he and Mr. McGee formed Cleckley and McGee, a commercial building construction firm. Mr. Cleckley served on the board of directors of the First National Bank for twenty years, from 1941 to 1961.

Mr. Cleckley was well known for his civic and church involvement. He was on the board of trustees of the Orangeburg Regional Hospital for many years, including two as its chairman. He was among the early members of the Rotary Club and remained active for almost forty years. From 1925 to 1930, he was a member of the Court House Commission, which was responsible for the relocation of the county courthouse from the town square as well as the construction of the new courthouse two blocks away. Mr. Cleckley served as an Orangeburg County commissioner from 1921 to 1925 by appointment of the legislature and also from 1932 to 1948 when it was by election of the people. The County Commission was the predecessor of our current County Council. He also served as president of the Orangeburg County Tuberculosis Association for twenty-five years.

Mr. Cleckley quietly provided financial assistance, making a college education possible for many young people. Even his own family did not know the extent of his philanthropy.

J.F. Cleckley was a bulwark in his church, the Union Methodist Church in Cope. He served as a steward for over forty years, a trustee for over thirty years, a Sunday school superintendent for many years and was a delegate to the South Carolina Annual Conference many times.

He married Julia Knotts of North in 1902, and they had one daughter: Margaret Cleckley Walter. He died in 1964 after a consummate career in the business world.

Laval David Dash (1878–1928)

As a child, Laval David Dash always wanted to work for himself. Being an African American farmer with a limited education around the turn of the twentieth century did not deter him. He saw a need and proceeded to fill the gap by establishing the first taxi service in Orangeburg.

At six feet, seven inches, he cast an imposing shadow that was only outdone by his determination and imagination in starting Orangeburg's first taxi service. He owned a handsome, high-stepping horse that provided the breakthrough for his new business. With the horse attached to a surrey, Mr. Dash started out transporting people to and from the railroad stations for their trips. Before the days of cars, trains were the only feasible mode of transportation between cities. As time went on, he would transport wedding parties on their "getaway" from the showering handfuls of a rice bombardment. Additionally, he began to provide a general taxi service for customers around town.

Dash took great pride in providing the customers with a sparkling clean surrey and horse, not to mention his dependable and courteous service. He was highly trusted and respected. As cars came on the scene, he, too, upgraded to a Model T Ford.

Unfortunately, on Christmas night in 1928, his wife found him dead beside his car after his last pickup of the day. He was coming home early to have a family Christmas celebration with his wife, five sons and three daughters.

His widow, Mattie Rufus Dash, immediately hired a driver until her oldest son, W.C., then thirteen, was granted special permission to drive a taxi. As time went on, all of the children participated in the business at one time or another, building it into a ten-cab fleet at its peak. Today, Dash's Taxi service is still in service, as it has been for almost 110 years.

Mr. and Mrs. Dash had eight children: Warren (W.C.), Rufus (Son Dash), Harvin, Johnson, Leon, Annie, Sadie and Barbara.

If hard work and sheer determination make for the success of a business, then Laval David Dash was the perfect example.

REVEREND DR. GEORGE E. DAVIS (1873–1928)

Reverend Dr. George Davis was the beloved pastor and leader of First Baptist Church in Orangeburg for twenty years before his untimely death in 1928.

Born in Baltimore, Maryland, in 1873 to Thomas B. and Josephine Magruder Davis, he received his early childhood education there. His college education was obtained at Hall Collegiate Institute, and he graduated from Crozier Theological Seminary in 1903.

Courtesy First Baptist Church.

He served several churches in West Virginia and Virginia until receiving the call to First Baptist Church in Orangeburg in 1908. The growth of the church during his twenty-year tenure was unprecedented. The membership grew from a mere 250 to nearly 1,400, and the sanctuary was enlarged to where it could seat 900. The Baraca Sunday School Class for men, which he personally taught, grew to over 200 members. A large three-story education and recreation building was built in 1926 and named the Davis Memorial Building. During his pastorate, 8 young men decided to enter the ministry, a testament to the strong religious guidance of Dr. Davis.

In 1926, Furman University conferred the doctor of divinity degree on Dr. Davis. He served as the chairman of the Orangeburg Baptist Association and on the general board of the Baptists of South Carolina, as well as many statewide committees.

First Baptist Church experienced tremendous growth and thrived under Dr. Davis's leadership. His dedication to his congregation and the city of Orangeburg was unparalleled.

Reverend Davis married the former Katherine Test in 1894, and they had two daughters and one son: Josephine Helen Davis Gullick, Jeanette Test Davis Latimer and Robert Davis. He died unexpectedly while visiting his daughter in Greenville in 1928.

Oliver C. Dawson (1910–1989)

Affectionately known as "Ollie the Man for All Seasons," Oliver C. Dawson was a coaching legend at South Carolina State University.

Mr. Dawson was born in 1910 in Thomaston, Georgia, and grew up in Cleveland, Ohio. He attended John Carroll University in Cleveland and

Courtesy Gracia Dawson.

graduated in 1936 from South Carolina State University. After receiving a master's degree from New York University in 1947, he did further postgraduate work at Denver University and West Virginia University.

Coach Dawson came to SC State in 1936 as an assistant football coach and became head coach in 1937, in which position he served until 1950. His team was undefeated in 1947 and played for the national championship for black colleges and universities.

During his forty-one-year career at SC State, he coached five sports and won conference championships in four of these: football, basketball, tennis and golf. He coached basketball for eleven seasons, track and field for four years and tennis for seven years. Coach Dawson founded the golf program and won four conference titles in his six seasons as coach.

He was chairman of the Department of Health and Physical Education for thirty years, as well as SC State's athletic director for sixteen years. Coach Dawson retired in 1976 after forty-one years of service to SC State University.

Mr. Dawson was elected to three athletic halls of fame: the South Carolina Athletic Hall of Fame in 1974, being the first African American elected there; a charter member of the SC State University Athletic Hall of Fame in 1983; and the John Carroll University Athletic Hall of Fame.

Because of his commitment and dedication to SC State's athletic programs through the years, the football stadium was named the Oliver C. Dawson Stadium in 1984.

Mr. Dawson was a member of many sports and professional organizations. He served on Orangeburg's Hillcrest Recreation Commission from its inception in 1972 until his death in 1989. Religiously, he belonged to St. Luke's Presbyterian Church, where he served as an elder and on the Presbyterian Men's Council.

Coach Dawson married Gracia Watermann, and they had one daughter: Maria Dawson James.

Former SC State president Dr. Maceo Nance summed it up best when he said, "Oliver Dawson was Mr. Athletics at S.C. State University." Coach Dawson was truly a coaching legend at his alma mater.

Andrew C. Dibble (1895–1982)

Andrew C. Dibble is the one person most responsible for making Edisto Memorial Gardens the horticultural splendor that exists today. When he began his dedicated work there in 1937, the gardens were already ten years old but had floundered somewhat up to that point. He is credited with creating and implementing his master plan that that has provided the grandeur that is now present.

Born in Orangeburg to Andrew Comstock Dibble and Rachel Agnes Clark Dibble, he was educated in the city schools here and then received a degree in horticulture from Clemson College in 1916. After working two years at the Taylor Plantation in Columbia to establish its pecan orchards, he returned to Clemson as an extension horticulturalist for two years. Dibble then came back to Orangeburg in 1920 with the hopes of becoming a commercial landscape and nursery operator, but his business was too slow to earn a living, so he went to work at Orangeburg National Bank. When the Depression closed the bank, he began operating his plant nursery again. Business was so slow that he would have to swap a plant for a ham, etc., to survive. He even landscaped two homes and contributed the plants in exchange for the client building Mr. Dibble's office at the nursery.

Courtesy Alex Dibble.

When the opportunity to become the city superintendent of parks came in 1937, he eagerly jumped at the job. Although Edisto Memorial Gardens was ten years old, it consisted of only a five-acre rose and azalea garden in boggy conditions as well as a playground for city children.

His refurbishment included raising the river dike and the azalea garden to keep the Edisto River from flooding all the azaleas, establishing a lake area, replacing the playground with a new rose garden area and establishing plants all along the hillside area across the road, as well as creating the picturesque garden drive there. Many additional flowering trees, shrubs and vines were propagated and planted to expand the gardens. The Chinese water wheel that has now become the signature landmark of the gardens was his creation also. He even drew plans for a water garden that ultimately became the boardwalk in the Horne Wetlands Park some thirty years after his retirement. Mr. Dibble also established the rose test garden for the All American Rose Society. His vision and perfection made Edisto Memorial Gardens the horticultural attraction it has become. Visitors from all over would come for the azalea blooming season. On Sundays during peak bloom, over ten thousand cars would drive through the gardens soaking up the beauty that Mr. Dibble created. He retired from his position in 1964 after twenty-seven years of making Edisto Memorial Gardens into a horticultural showcase.

In 1921, he married the former Lucille Jackson, and they had four sons: Andrew, Jack, Lewis and Robert. He died in 1982.

THOMAS ORMAND SUMMERS DIBBLE (1859–1935)

T.O.S. Dibble was born in Charleston in 1859 to Philander Virgil Dibble and Frances Ann Dibble. His family moved to Orangeburg during the Civil War.

Mr. Dibble served as a captain of the local militia, known as the Edisto Rifles, for thirty years. He was a member of the Young America volunteer fire department, serving as its chief for many years. Additionally, he was the chief of all the city's volunteer fire departments for many years. Mr. Dibble also served as secretary of the State Firemen's Association.

Mr. Dibble was long involved in Masonry, serving as the worshipful master of the Shibboleth Lodge here from 1882 to 1884 and as its secretary for an additional twenty-five years. He was also a member of the local lodge of the Elks. Mr. Dibble was an officer of the Red Shirts, an organization loyal to General Wade Hampton, who opposed the Radical Regime in South Carolina government.

He was also an active member of the Episcopal Church of the Redeemer and was made a warden emeritus.

In 1913 he ascended to the office of Orangeburg city clerk and treasurer, in which position he served for twenty-two years until his death.

Mr. Dibble married Winnie P. Wightman, and they had four children: Samuel W. Dibble, Mrs. Ed M. Mowry, Miss Susie Dibble and Mrs. W.O. Young.

As a fitting tribute to his long-standing career as a fireman and fire chief, the ladder truck, adorned in floral splendor, carried his casket to his funeral and burial in 1935. The hour of the funeral was tolled by the fire bell on the truck during the entire service.

W. Hampton Dukes (1867–1947)

Mr. W. Hampton Dukes established what is now the long-standing funeral service establishment in Orangeburg, Dukes-Harley Funeral Home, in 1896.

Hampy Dukes was born in 1867, one of fourteen children born to John Henry and Sophia Dukes in Orangeburg. He was named for his father's former cavalry commander, General Wade Hampton.

Mr. Dukes was educated in Orangeburg and was an avid baseball player, having played on a local all-star team called the Orangeburg Diamonds that played against teams from other towns and cities.

He graduated from Professor J.H. Clark's School of Embalming in 1895. In 1896, he established the Dukes Undertaking Company on St. John Street near the county jail. His business was granted one of the first licenses in South Carolina issued to embalmers. For the first several years, he was the only licensed embalming firm between Columbia and Charleston. In that day and time, all funerals were conducted with horse buggies and carriages. Additionally, he sold marble and granite tombstones for cemetery graves.

Courtesy St. Paul's United Methodist Church.

Mr. Dukes was a past president of the South Carolina Funeral Directors and Embalmers Association. He was a member of the Rotary Club, as well as being a member of the Knights of Pythias and the Woodmen of the World. He was very active in civic affairs in Orangeburg. Religiously, he was a lifelong member of St. Paul's Methodist Church.

Upon his retirement, Clifton and I.S. Harley continued his funeral business as the Dukes-Harley Funeral Home, which is now celebrating over one hundred years of offering funeral services in Orangeburg.

Mr. Dukes was an avid fisherman and was well known for the fish fries he held. He even had a custom-made cast-iron frying pan for these events that measured over three feet in diameter.

Mr. Dukes married the former Agnes Lightfoot and they had two daughters: Mrs. G.E. Rhodes and Mrs. R.C. Leslie. He died in 1947.

GEORGE HERMAN FISCHER (1893–1945)

Herman Fischer served as Orangeburg's first fire chief after the City of Orangeburg took over the firefighting responsibilities from the volunteer fire departments in May 1920.

Mr. Fischer was born in 1893 to Augustus S. and Elizabeth B. Fischer. His father was the chief of police in Orangeburg for many years. Herman received his education in the public schools of Orangeburg. He was a veteran of World War I and a member of the American Legion.

Courtesy Orangeburg County Historical Society.

After being a leader in one of the volunteer fire departments, he was chosen in May 1920 to be the first fire chief for the City of Orangeburg when all the volunteer fire departments were consolidated into one city department. He served with distinction in this capacity until his sudden death in 1945. Chief Fischer was a leader in the South Carolina Fireman's Association and served as its president in the 1930s.

Chief Fischer was highly praised for bringing the new fire department from its fledgling status to one of the finest in the country. His progressive methods with techniques and firefighting equipment were highly commended. He was always implementing new improvements to provide the finest fire service possible.

During World War II, he was called upon to develop plans for the firefighting defenses of South Carolina against the possibility of air raid damage.

Mr. Fischer married Veronica Brunson, and they had two children: George H. Fischer Jr. and Marjorie Fischer. He died in 1945. At his funeral at the Orangeburg Lutheran Church, the city fire bell tolled at thirty-second intervals during the entire service out of respect for this dedicated and devoted leader.

Flora Ella "Florella" Fordham (1880–1973)

As a child growing up, all Florella Fordham wanted to do was become a nurse. She achieved her dream and returned to Orangeburg as our first registered nurse (RN) in 1903.

Born to John Hammond and Louisa Smith Fordham, Florella Fordham grew up in Orangeburg in a prominent family. She always wanted to be a nurse but met considerable resistance from her parents with her dream. But her persistence paid off, and she went to Hampton Institute in Virginia following her 1900 graduation from Claflin College. After graduating with her RN degree in 1903, she returned to Orangeburg and started her legendary career.

Courtesy Louisa Robinson.

There was no hospital in Orangeburg at the time, and she immediately became a favorite of all the doctors here. She would go from house to house to tend the sick in their homes. Her deepest affection was delivering babies, which numbered about five hundred during her illustrious career. She would walk from case to case at all hours of the day and night, her nurse's cape flowing in the breeze.

In 1932, South Carolina State University needed a resident

nurse, and Florella was hired to fill that position. She remained there for twenty years, retiring in 1952. However, her alma mater, Claflin, then convinced her to become its resident nurse, and she remained there for seven more years. When Florella retired for good in 1959, she had dedicated fifty-six years of her life to helping others, becoming truly a legend in the field of nursing.

In the 1930s, Miss Fordham helped organize the Licensed Practical Nursing program in Orangeburg and helped teach there too. Because of her dedication to healing the sick, she never found time to consider marriage.

Florella was a devout member of Trinity Methodist Church. After a long and distinguished career in nursing, she died in 1973.

DANIEL OSCAR HERBERT (1857–1930)

Daniel Oscar Herbert was a well-known attorney and bank president in Orangeburg.

He was born in Newberry County in 1857 to Captain C.W. and Elizabeth Groggins Herbert. He received his undergraduate degree from Wofford College in 1878 as well as a master of arts degree there in 1879. In 1881, he graduated from Vanderbilt University's law school and was admitted to the bar the following year.

Courtesy Rosenger.

From 1887 to 1890, he served as the U.S. Post Office inspector, spending much time in New England and on the Pacific coast. In 1890, he came to Orangeburg to practice law in the firm of Izlar, Glaze, and Herbert.

In 1898, he helped raise a military company for the Edisto Rifles for the Spanish-American War and served as its captain. They served in Columbia, Savannah and ultimately Cuba during this conflict. After the war, he continued his military career in the State Militia and became colonel of the Second Regiment of the South Carolina National Guard. He also served on the staff of Governor Duncan C. Heyward. From 1902 to 1906, he was a member of the South Carolina House of Representatives and became closely associated with future governor John G. Richards. Mr. Herbert also served on Orangeburg's City Council from 1899 to 1901 and on the local board of education.

Mr. Herbert was a founder of People's Bank and was its attorney. Additionally, he served as its president for many years. After its consolidation with Orangeburg National Bank, he continued there as president. He was also president of the General Land and Investment Company.

Religiously, Mr. Herbert was a very active member of St. Paul's Methodist Church, where he served as a faithful choir member, on the board of stewards and as a member of the trustees.

In 1893, he married Miss Julia Salley of Orangeburg, and they had six children: Alexander S. Herbert, Mary Herbert Raysor, Walter Herbert, Daniel Oscar Herbert Jr., Sallie Herbert and Julia Herbert. Mr. Herbert died in 1930.

Judge Jerry M. Hughes (1884–1970)

Judge Jerry M. Hughes is a sterling example of longevity and dedicated service. He was the probate judge in Orangeburg County for fifty-four years and was the general manager of the Orangeburg County Fair Association for fifty-nine years.

Jerry Miles Hughes was born in the Fork section of Orangeburg County between Cope and Cordova in 1884 to J. Miles and Margaret M. Hughes. His education was obtained at the old Sheridan School on Amelia Street and at Orangeburg High School. After that, he graduated from the University of South Carolina and later its law school in 1907. After opening a law office in Orangeburg, he left to go to the new state of Oklahoma, selling real estate for two years before returning to teach school for one year at a one-room country school in Livingston. But his love of the law prevailed, and he returned to his Orangeburg law practice.

In 1911, an event occurred that would change Mr. Hughes's life forever. The Orangeburg County Fair Association was formed to showcase agricultural exhibits and provide amusement for the people. He was elected secretary and treasurer. As secretary, he was the overall general manager of the fair, a position he held for fifty-nine years until his death in 1970.

Courtesy Orangeburg County Fair Association.

Additionally, in 1951, he was elected president of the fair association. As the person in charge of the fair, his word was his bond. A handshake from Judge Hughes was as good as a written contract. During his fifty-nine years in charge, he would quietly roam the fairgrounds keenly observing the people's reactions. He was the innovator who would then tailor the fair to the visitors' needs.

Sports, especially football, were dear to Judge Hughes's heart. He started the "Big Friday" college football games during the fair week in the 1910s that featured teams like the University of South Carolina, Clemson, The Citadel, Wofford and Newberry College. This tradition continued through the 1950s. Of course, the fairgrounds stadium was home to his beloved Orangeburg High School football team. As a fitting tribute to Judge Hughes and his promotion of football at the fairgrounds, the approximately five-thousand-seat stadium was named Judge Hughes Stadium in the early 1960s.

In 1916, Mr. Hughes was elected as Orangeburg County's judge of probate, a position he held for fifty-four years. He was also president of Home Building and Loan Association in Orangeburg.

Fraternally, Judge Hughes was a member of the Knights of Pythias, serving as grand prelate and grand chancellor. He was also a member of the Rotary Club for forty years.

Judge Hughes married Iressie Collier, and they had three sons: Jerry Jr., Thomas and William. He died in 1970.

OCTAVIA M. JENNINGS (1873–1949)

There were no civic or patriotic endeavors in Orangeburg in which Octavia Jennings did not take an active part. She truly was one of the finest civic servants to have graced the city of Orangeburg.

Courtesy Orangeburg County Historical Society.

Octavia "Tavie" Moses Jennings was born in 1873 in Sumter to Perry and Rosa L. Moses, a prominent Sumter family. After her marriage in 1895 to Robert H. Jennings Sr., she moved to Orangeburg.

Possessing a charming and caring personality, she was considered to be a great lady by everyone who came in contact with her. In 1896, she was a charter member of the Dixie Club, which developed into one of the finest charitable organizations around. Created at first as a ladies' book club, it evolved into Orangeburg's first library with over twenty-five thousand volumes. She also served as its president. She also was a leader in the Orangeburg Garden Club and led community efforts for everyone to beautify their yards as well as public places.

When Orangeburg's first hospital was established in 1919, she organized the Hospital Relief Association to help raise funds for charity care there as well as served as its leader for many years. When the three area counties took over this private hospital in 1934, she served as an able member of its board of trustees for many years. Mrs. Jennings was also a member of the Moultrie Chapter of the Daughters of the American Revolution and the Paul McMichael Chapter of the United Daughters of the Confederacy and served on the board of the Tamassee DAR School. During World War I, she was involved in every aspect of the American Red Cross in this area. She liberally supported many charitable causes in Orangeburg.

Mrs. Jennings and her husband had one son: Robert H. "Bob" Jennings Jr. She died in 1949 after a long life of devotion to the people of Orangeburg.

Robert H. Jennings Sr. (1869–1943)

Robert H. Jennings Sr. was an accomplished businessman in Orangeburg as well as an energetic civic leader. He also served as our progressive mayor for four terms from 1921 to 1937.

Courtesy City of Orangeburg.

Robert H. Jennings Sr. was born near Dalzell in Sumter County in 1869 to James M. and Teresa Yates Jennings. His education was obtained in the public schools in Sumter County. His early employment was as a bookkeeper in Sumter. In the late 1890s, he moved to Orangeburg and later established a wholesale grocery business, Jennings and Smoak, in 1898. This partnership also operated one of the largest plantations in the county. In 1910, he and Perry Smoak started the Orangeburg Fertilizer Company. They also established the Orangeburg Coca-Cola Bottling Co., along with W.S. Barton and Fletcher Fairey. Additionally, he and Mr. Smoak purchased the Peoples Baking Co., which later became Palmetto Baking Co., which later produced the popular Sunbeam line of products, and also the Orangeburg Ice and Fuel Co.

Civically, Mr. Jennings was a dynamo. He was the president of the Chamber of Commerce, also known as the Young Men's Business League, for the first seven years of its existence. He was a perennial leader and a chairman of the Orangeburg Fall Festival, which was a precursor to the Orangeburg County Fair. In addition to his business interests, he also served as our police chief for a while. Mr. Jennings also was one of the community leaders in the efforts to establish our first hospital in the 1910s.

Mr. Jennings was also active in Democratic Party politics. He was a delegate to the Democratic National Convention in 1920 and served as the chairman of the Orangeburg County Democratic Executive Committee from 1924 to 1929.

Fraternally, Mr. Jennings was a past master of the Shibboleth Masonic temple, a Knights Templar, a member of the Mystic Shrine, exalted ruler of the Elks and a member of the Knights of Pythias.

In 1895, he married the former Octavia "Tavie" Moses from Sumter, and they had one son: Robert "Bob" Jennings Jr. Mr. Jennings died in 1943 after a long illness.

Robert H. Jennings Sr. was a mover and a shaker in helping Orangeburg progress from a sleepy little town into a thriving city. His energy expended and his leadership skills to make Orangeburg thrive were unparalleled.

Robert H. Jennings Jr. (1896–1962)

As a successful businessman and a very progressive mayor, Bob Jennings led Orangeburg in an era of tremendous growth.

Born in 1896 to Robert H. and Octavia M. Jennings in Orangeburg, he attended the public schools here in his formative years. He also attended Porter Military Academy in Charleston and later Clemson College. In 1916, he enlisted in the United States Army and served along the Mexican border first and then later as a lieutenant on the battlefront in France in World War I.

After returning from his military service, Mr. Jennings joined his father's business enterprises here in Orangeburg. As his business successes progressed, he became president of Palmetto Baking Co., the Orangeburg Ice and Fuel Co. and the Orangeburg Coca-Cola Bottling Co., as well as vice-president of Orangeburg Building and Loan Association. He was also a member of the board of directors of First National Bank. In 1928, he served as the president of the Southern Bakers Association.

Bob Jennings, like his father, was a progressive mayor, serving for twelve years. His dynamic leadership produced an improved city airport facility, the relocation of Highway 301 to keep from clogging our main street, significant improvements in Edisto Memorial Gardens and totally reconstructing the square downtown, among the many projects he led. Our city-owned airport was named Jennings Field in his honor.

Courtesy City of Orangeburg.

Fraternally, Mr. Jennings was a member and past president of the Rotary Club, a past exalted ruler of the Elks, a Mason, a Shriner and a member of the American

Legion and the VFW. Religiously, he was an active member of the Episcopal Church of the Redeemer.

"Mr. Bob," as he was known around town, was also a generous philanthropist. Despite his gruff exterior in his business activities, he had a deep caring for his fellow man. He gave significantly to many causes. Among these was helping many young people financially in attending college. He always regretted not finishing college himself, and this was his way of helping others. There were many students from Orangeburg who never will know that it was Bob Jennings's contributions that enabled them to attend college.

Mr. Jennings married Clem Buchanan, and they had one son: Robert H. Jennings III. After Mrs. Jennings's death, he married Jean H. Stroman in 1948. Mr. Jennings died in 1962.

Businessman, civic leader, philanthropist, Bob Jennings will always be remembered for making Orangeburg a better place in which to live.

ROBERT LIDE (1871–1944)

Eminent lawyer, statesman, banker and philanthropist, Robert Lide has been a solid rock in Orangeburg's history.

Mr. Lide was born in 1871 to Reverend Thomas P. and Martha H. Lide in Greenville. Because of his father's ministry, he grew up in several different towns in North and South Carolina. He received an AB degree from Wake Forest College in 1892. Afterward, he studied law in Orangeburg under B. Hart Moss and was admitted to the bar in 1894. He then entered into a law partnership with Mr. Moss.

Mr. Lide began his career in public service in 1895 when he became a United States commissioner. From 1900 to 1904, he was a member of the South Carolina House of Representatives. In 1908, he was elected as Orangeburg County's senator, serving until 1916. Mr. Lide was elected Orangeburg's mayor from 1917 to 1919. From 1904 to 1914, he was the Orangeburg County Democratic Party chairman and was a delegate to the national convention in St. Louis in 1916. Mr. Lide also served as chairman of the Orangeburg County Court House Commission, which was responsible for building the new courthouse in 1927.

Additionally, Mr. Lide was a highly regarded correspondent for twelve years for the Charleston daily newspaper, the *News and Courier*. He was a member of the Orangeburg County Board of Education as well as a member of the board of trustees for Furman University.

Courtesy Jean Harrison.

In the business world, he helped organize three small-town banks in Fort Motte, Elloree and Holly Hill, becoming president of each of these. In 1934, he helped organize the First National Bank in Orangeburg (now SCB&T) and was president for several years until his death in 1944.

Mr. Lide was selected as a special judge on several occasions and even sat with the South Carolina Supreme Court. He also served as president of the Orangeburg County Bar Association.

He was a past president of the Rotary Club and held offices in the Knights of Pythias and the Woodmen of the World, as well as being a member of the Elks. Religiously, Mr. Lide was a dedicated member of the First Baptist Church and was the chairman of the board of deacons there.

Mr. Lide was also a member of the board of trustees of the Tri-County Hospital in Orangeburg. It was through his generosity that 1,500 volumes of medical books were purchased for the hospital medical library. After his death, the library became known as the Robert Lide Memorial Library.

In 1897, Mr. Lide married the former Ethel M. Lowman, and they had three daughters: Mildred L. Fair, Evelyn L. Glenn and Ethel L. Council. After a long and distinguished career of public service, Robert Lide died in 1944.

William A. Livingston (1881–1971)

W.A. Livingston was one of Orangeburg's most respected and prominent businessmen. He was a very involved civic leader as well as a mayor of Orangeburg.

Mr. Livingston was born in Orangeburg in 1881 to Henry W. and Harriett P. Livingston. He received his education in Orangeburg as well as

Courtesy City of Orangeburg.

at a private school in Georgia. In 1898, he volunteered to serve in the Spanish-American War and was stationed in Cuba.

Upon his return from the war, he worked as a bookkeeper for three years prior to being a traveling representative for the Southern Fruit Company of Charleston. In 1914, he started his own fruit and produce business in Orangeburg. He later spread into groceries and metal products.

In 1914, Mr. Livingston was elected president of the state chapter of the Travelers Protective Association and in 1917 was president of the Orangeburg Chamber of Commerce. In 1919, he was elected to fill the unexpired term of Robert Lide as mayor of Orangeburg. During his tenure, an $800,000 bond was issued to add significant improvements to Orangeburg in the form of sewer extensions, street paving, sidewalks, street curbing and new electric streetlights along Russell and Broughton Streets. Also, all the volunteer fire departments were merged into a new city-owned department with paid firemen.

Mr. Livingston was a charter member of the Rotary Club in 1921 and later served as its president. He was also a member of the local school board in the 1920s and served as its chairman. During World War II, he was chairman of the Tri-County Hospital's board of trustees.

Mr. Livingston also served as president of the United States Wholesale Grocers Association for two terms. He was instrumental in forming the forerunner of the South Carolina State Chamber of Commerce and served as its president. He was also president of the South Carolina Motor Transport Association for two terms.

Mr. Livingston was also a member of the board of directors of the Citizens and Southern National Bank of Charleston and the Colonial Life and Accident Insurance Company. In 1967, Mr. Livingston was selected as the

"Citizen of the Year" for Orangeburg because of his lifelong commitment to Orangeburg.

W.A. Livingston married the former Lurline Crum, and they had three daughters: Nonie, Annie Lee and Lurline. He died in 1971 after a long and distinguished business and civic career. He was noted to be a man "sharp of mind, fair in business dealings, a brilliant conversationalist, and a keen analytical mind."

Daniel H. Marchant (1854–1938)

Daniel H. Marchant could be considered the music king of Orangeburg. His Marchant's Music Company in town was the place to buy pianos and organs when music played a prevalent role in households in the late 1800s and early 1900s.

Mr. Marchant was born in Graniteville in 1854 and came to Orangeburg in 1881, where he was employed in the large mercantile business of Mr. George H. Cornelson. Because of his love of music, he opened a music store on the side in 1882 where he sold pianos and other musical instruments. After ten years with Mr. Cornelson, he opened a shoe store for several years before going full time in the music business in 1897. The Marchant Music Co. thrived for many years, and Mr. Marchant worked until three weeks before his death at age eighty-four. At its peak, he employed two sons, two outside salesmen, a piano tuner and one or two young ladies to play selections for customers. Outside of Charleston, he operated the largest music store in the state. Mr. Marchant sold everything from pianos and organs, to jew's-harps, to phonographs,

Courtesy Yates Snowden, History of South Carolina.

not to mention sheet music, music books and strings for all kinds of stringed instruments. Player pianos even proved to be popular after their advent.

Mr. Marchant was an avid traveler, visiting all but two states in the nation. Internationally, he traveled to five of the seven continents. At age seventy-two, he took a grand tour abroad, where he visited southern Europe and northern Africa, where he rode camels to the pyramids, boated down the Nile, toured Jerusalem and tobogganed in the Madeira Islands.

At St. Paul's Methodist Church, Mr. Marchant was the leader of the choir for twenty-seven years and led the singing in his Sunday school class for an equal number of years. Additionally, he served on the board of stewards for fifty-two years, being its chairman as well as its secretary and treasurer for many years.

Mr. Marchant married the former Julia Ann Bond from Georgia, and they had four children: Daniel H. Marchant Jr., W.W. Marchant, Leila M. Smith and Julia Belle M. Culler. He died in 1938 after a long career in a music-filled life.

John Moreau Maxwell Sr. (1881–1938)

Maxwell's Staple and Fancy Groceries was considered by many to be the finest grocery store in Orangeburg. Known for its exceptional service and quality groceries, Maxwell's served clientele who were substantial citizens from both racial groups.

Born in 1881 in Augusta, Georgia, John Maxwell was the son of Henry Johnson Maxwell and his wife, Martha Louisa Dibble Maxwell. He grew up in Sumter County and attended Mather Academy. Mr. Maxwell had his college preparatory education at Claflin University and is thought to have gone there for his college education too. He attended Meharry Dental School but became ill and had to withdraw.

John Maxwell apprenticed as a young man with his uncle John M. Dibble in Camden at his grocery business. Camden was a winter resort for wealthy northerners, and the patrons of Dibble's were from high social and economic circles. As a result, the store stocked many gourmet and fancy type groceries. The experience John Maxwell obtained there propelled his desire to open his own grocery store in Orangeburg in 1904. Maxwell's Staple and Fancy Groceries was located first on Railroad Avenue (now Webber Boulevard) and moved three years later to East Russell Street between Railroad Avenue and Treadwell Street.

Courtesy E. Louise, Naudin-Dibble Heritage Foundation Collection.

Maxwell's preeminent characteristic was its ability to provide quality service in addition to the fancy lines it carried. Prominent citizens, both black and white, patronized this exceptional establishment.

After John Maxwell's death in 1938, his family continued the operation of his store until 1951. In 1940, it employed six clerks, one bookkeeper, four delivery boys and additional personnel during weekends and holidays.

John Maxwell married the former Katherine Louise Cardozo, who was the daughter of Reverend Isaac Nunez Cardozo, a pastor at Trinity Methodist Church and professor at Claflin University and State A&M College. They had six children: John M. Maxwell Jr., Cassandra E. Maxwell, Nunez C. Maxwell, Katherine M. Vincent, Dr. Charles W. Maxwell II and Henry C. Maxwell. Mr. Maxwell is buried in historic Orangeburg Cemetery.

Reverend John Logan McLees (1855–1925)

Reverend John L. McLees was the much beloved pastor of the First Presbyterian Church in Orangeburg for thirty-six years.

Reverend McLees was born in 1855 in Greenwood to Reverend John and Sarah McLees. Because of the depressed economy following the Civil War, his father was forced to farm in addition to his pastoral duties to make ends meet. After working on the family farm growing up, Mr. McLees entered Adger College in Walhalla, where he graduated in 1879. He often said that he wore the same suit of clothes on his graduation day that he wore on the day he entered college. For the next two years, he taught school in Brunswick, Georgia. In 1881, he entered Columbia Theological Seminary and, with much denial in life, graduated in 1885. He was licensed to preach

Courtesy Yates Snowden, History of South Carolina.

and was ordained that same year. He then served in Providence and Charlotte, North Carolina, for the next four years. Reverend McLees received the call to the pastorate at First Presbyterian Church in Orangeburg in 1889, where he faithfully served for the next thirty-six years until his death. Additionally, he helped St. Matthews organize a Presbyterian church and would go fourteen miles by horse and buggy every Sunday afternoon for over twelve years to minister to them. What compensation he received for doing so was given back so they could erect their first church.

Reverend McLees was in high demand for revivals and other occasions at numerous churches in the county. He was noted for being able to deliver his messages in a happy vein with good humor.

As time went on, Reverend McLees established a large 1,200-acre farm outside Orangeburg. He also became a director of the People's National Bank, which later became known as Orangeburg National Bank. Reverend McLees was chairman of the board of trustees for Chicora College for Women (located then in Columbia and now known as Queen's University in Charlotte). He was also involved civically in the Rotary Club.

In 1893, he married Annie L. Cornelson, daughter of one of Orangeburg's most prominent businessmen, George Cornelson, and his wife, Angie. They had five children: Angie M. McMichael, Sarah M. Elliott, George C. McLees, John L. McLees Jr. and Arthur McLees. Reverend McLees died in 1925. As a giant in the South Carolina Presbyterian church, his funeral was conducted by the president of Chicora College and the head of Columbia Theological Seminary. Most businesses in Orangeburg suspended their operations during the hour of his funeral as a tribute to one of Orangeburg's finest citizens.

Dr. E. Benjamin McTeer (1889–1967)

Dr. Ben McTeer was a noted African American dentist in Orangeburg. He practiced here for forty-five years until his death at age seventy-seven.

Dr. McTeer was born in 1889 in Orangeburg County to Dr. Asbury Benjamin and Essie Levin McTeer. Unfortunately, his mother died in childbirth, and he was reared by his maternal grandmother. He attended the Branchville schools and graduated from Claflin University. He attended dental school at Howard University in Washington and graduated from there in 1922.

Dr. McTeer's grandmother emphasized character, ethics, hard work and religious faith during his formative years. At a young age, he began working at the Sulton Lumber Company. Because of his hard work ethic, he was given increasingly responsible jobs. It was through the Sultons that he received the opportunity to attend Claflin University. He continued to work weekends and vacations for the Sultons. After college, "Mack" went to New York to earn money to help go to dental school by being a Pullman porter on the Buffalo to New York run. While at dental school, he worked nights at the U.S. Government Printing Office. He also served for several months in the army. After his 1922 graduation, he returned to Orangeburg to begin his dental practice. Times were tough at first, but he persevered, and he practiced until 1967.

Courtesy Miriam Abernathy.

As a dentist, he was known for his caring attitude. If a patient in pain knocked on his door at 2:00 a.m., he would get up and go to the office to relieve the pain. As telephones were not widely used, he did not have a home phone for his first thirty years of practice.

Dr. McTeer married Claudia Geneva White, and they had two children: Dr. William Austin McTeer and Dr. Miriam McTeer Abernathy. He died in

1967 at age seventy-seven, seven weeks after suffering a severe heart attack. "Mack" had performed sixteen extractions on the day of his heart attack.

EDWARD V. MIRMOW (1900–1995)

Mr. Eddie Mirmow would have to be considered one of the biggest sports enthusiasts ever in Orangeburg. As a tribute to his contributions to sports, our municipal baseball stadium is named Mirmow Field.

Eddie Mirmow was born in New York City in 1900 to Russian immigrants, Morris and Tannie Mirmow. In 1901, the family moved to Orangeburg, where Eddie remained until his death. He was educated in our local schools and was on the first Orangeburg High School football team in 1913. Mr. Mirmow graduated from the University of South Carolina, where he lettered in both football and baseball.

For many years, Mr. Mirmow's side yard was used as a football and baseball field for all the neighborhood kids. After World War II, Mr. Mirmow reorganized the Orangeburg American Legion Post 4 baseball program. In 1948, he led the efforts to establish a city-owned baseball stadium. City Council unanimously voted to name it Mirmow Field because of his sports dedication in Orangeburg. This ball field hosted the 1966 American Legion World Series for the entire United States. Mr. Mirmow was the American Legion athletic director for many years, being responsible for the team and all the equipment. Often he would put players up in his home after night games when teams were few in the state, as they lived far away.

Mr. Mirmow founded the Orangeburg High School Indian Booster Club in 1946, which was the first high school booster club in the Southeast. It was also the largest booster club in the state for many years and boasted 657 members in 1959.

Courtesy SCB&T.

Mr. Mirmow operated Mirmow's Clothing Store until 1939, when he formed the Mid State Investment Company, where he remained until age eighty. He was a founder of First National Bank in 1934 and served as a director for the rest of his life. He also was a charter member of the Country Club of Orangeburg and the Rotary Club as well as a founding member of his synagogue, Temple Sinai.

Mr. Mirmow attended all the University of South Carolina home football games until age ninety-two.

He also attended many local sporting events, especially going to legion baseball games at Mirmow Field well into his nineties. He even played golf into his nineties.

He married the former Rebecca Blatt, and they had one son, Edward V. "Hank" Mirmow Jr. Mr. Mirmow died in 1995 after a lifetime of sports enthusiasm in Orangeburg.

Dr. Charles A. Mobley (1888–1973)

Dr. Charles A. Mobley made a lasting contribution to Orangeburg by establishing the first hospital here in 1919. As a skilled surgeon, he performed many miracles in his career.

Dr. Mobley was born in 1888 in Rock Hill to Fred and Anna Hope Mobley. He received his education at Rock Hill and the University of Tennessee before graduating from the Medical College of South Carolina in Charleston in 1910. He then completed a surgical residency in Rock Hill under Dr. W.W. Fennell.

Determined to start his own hospital, Dr. Mobley came to Orangeburg in 1919 to start the first hospital in the city. He converted a former dormitory at the site of the former Orangeburg Collegiate Institute into a twenty-five-bed hospital. Within six years, he had to erect another building in front, which increased the capacity to seventy beds. Dr. Mobley also established a nurses' training school to provide for the nursing needs at his hospital. There are many stories circulating about the many miracles he performed during his surgery career here.

Courtesy Regional Medical Center.

Dr. Mobley was a fellow of the American College of

Surgeons and was a charter member of the American Board of Surgery in 1937. He studied extensively each year at eminent institutions around the country to further his skills.

Dr. Mobley was a member of the board of directors of the First National Bank. His civic service was through the Rotary Club.

He married the former Susan Bailey from Edisto Island, and they had one son, Charles A. Mobley Jr., who died in 1947. After Mrs. Mobley's death in 1959, he married his brother's widow, Virginia Cork Mobley. After a brilliant career in surgery, Dr. Mobley died in 1973.

Orangeburg is forever grateful to Dr. Charles A. Mobley for establishing the first hospital here as well as ably serving our residents with the finest surgical care available.

JUDGE B. HART MOSS (1862–1939)

Lawyer, banker, judge—B. Hart Moss epitomized the consummate public servant. At his funeral, he was extolled for his exemplary life, his impeccable character and the outstanding influence he exerted over the Orangeburg community.

Courtesy Tony Emanuel.

B. Hart Moss was born in Orangeburg in 1862 to William Crawford and Rebecca Raysor Moss. He attended the Orangeburg schools and graduated from Wofford College in 1883. Afterward, he read law under Samuel Dibble and then practiced law with Robert Lide in the firm of Moss and Lide for thirty years until this firm became Raysor, Moss, and Lide in 1924. In 1925, he was elected to be the first Orangeburg County court judge and held that position for fourteen years until his death.

From a military standpoint, he served as captain of a local militia, the Dibble Light Dragoons, for several years. In 1899, he was elected to the South Carolina House of

Representatives and voluntarily stepped down after one term. For a number of years, he served as president of the Orangeburg County Bar Association. Additionally, he was counsel for the Democratic Party nominees in federal elections and was considered to be an authority in this type of law.

In local business, Mr. Moss was president of the Edisto National Bank for thirty years. It was said that when the stock market crash occurred and most banks failed in the aftermath, he personally reimbursed the bank's depositors from his own funds. He was also president of the Orangeburg Knitting Mill and vice-president of the Orangeburg Manufacturing Company.

Mr. Moss was a firm believer in quality education and served on the local school board for many years. Additionally, he was a longtime member of Wofford College's board of trustees and was its chairman at the time of his death. Quietly, he provided funds for many young men and women to attend college.

Judge Moss was very active at St. Paul's Methodist Church, where he served as assistant Sunday school superintendent and was on the board of stewards as well as being its chairman.

Judge Moss married the former Agnes Dibble, daughter of Congressman Samuel Dibble, in 1892, and they had three children: S. Dibble Moss, Mrs. John W. Harris and Agnes Moss. He died in 1939 after a long and distinguished career serving the people of Orangeburg.

Reverend Nelson C. Nix (1865–1944)

As a leader at South Carolina State University from the day of its opening, and as the longtime minister of Mount Pisgah Baptist Church, Nelson Nix cast a formidable shadow in Orangeburg.

Reverend Nix was born in 1865 in Barnwell County to Allen Nix and Charity Gilliard. As a boy, he attended school there. In 1890, he completed the normal course at Claflin University. His college education was divided between Benedict College in Columbia and Claflin, and he received an AB degree at Claflin. In 1907, both Claflin and Benedict conferred the doctor of divinity degree upon him. Reverend Nix also completed further graduate work at the University of Chicago.

In 1896, when the Colored Normal, Industrial, Agricultural and Mechanical College of South Carolina was formed, he became a member of the faculty and was head of the Mathematics Department. Later, he was made dean of the entire college, a position he held for many years until his death in 1944.

Courtesy of Orangeburg Consolidated School District 5.

Reverend Nix began preaching when he was about twenty-five years old and became ordained in 1894. He ably served several churches through the years. Among these were Andrew's Chapel, Mount Olive, Beauty Hill and Gethsemane. In 1902, he began a forty-two-year service as pastor of Mount Pisgah Baptist Church in Orangeburg.

Nelson Nix also operated a large two-hundred-acre farm near Norway for many years. In Orangeburg, he had a comfortable large home on Amelia Street at the corner of Treadwell. After his death, this house was used by the Catholic Church for over fifty years, primarily as a residence for the Xaverian Brothers order for their work with the church mission here.

For his many years of contributions to education, an elementary school was named Nix Elementary School in his memory.

Dr. Nix married Sylvia Robinson from Orangeburg, and they had four children: Bertha N. Waller, James Nix, Robert N.C. Nix and Lawrence M. Nix. Dr. Nix's legacy continued through his son Robert N.C. Nix, who lived his adult life in Pennsylvania and was the first African American congressman in the United States Congress in 1937, where he served for twenty-one years. In turn, Representative Nix's son was on the Pennsylvania Supreme Court for twenty-four years and served as chief justice for twelve of those years.

Reverend Dr. Nix died in 1944 after a lifetime of service to what is now South Carolina State University and the church.

JOHN F. PEARSON (1890–1968)

John F. Pearson was the legendary force behind the city of Orangeburg's public utility system. He was also the father of rural electrification, as his testimony in Washington led to the formation of the Rural Electrification Administration in America.

Courtesy Department of Public Utilities.

John Franklin Pearson was born in 1890 to Porter F. Pearson and Lorena Ann Bonnette Pearson in the Pinehill community. In 1909, he graduated from Orangeburg High School and in 1913 from Clemson College with a degree in mechanical and electrical engineering.

Mr. Pearson's working career began immediately after college in 1913 with the City of Orangeburg's Water and Light Department (now DPU). From 1915 to 1919 he served as the superintendent of the Blackville Light Co. He returned to Orangeburg in 1919 as the superintendent of the Water and Light Department, a position he held for the next thirty-seven years. When he started, the department had twelve employees and one mule and wagon. When he retired in 1956, the department had progressed to sixty employees and eighteen vehicles. In his early days, the legendary mule Liza amazed everyone. If Mr. Pearson was working in one area of town and needed the mule and wagon, he would get on his bicycle and ride there, put his bike in the wagon and go back to the needed site. When he finished, he would get on his bike and ride off, and Liza would then return on his own to the previous work site.

In the 1920s, Orangeburg had much pressure placed on it by big power companies that wanted to buy its city system. Mr. Pearson was vehemently opposed to this, even though he was promised lucrative positions with these companies. Thus, our Department of Public Utilities now ranks as one of the best models of local utilities in the state.

When Mr. Pearson arrived in 1919, the Water and Light Department was losing $1,000 a month. At the end of his first year, it made $21,000. By the time he retired from DPU in 1956, more than $4 million total had been turned over to the city, which resulted in lower taxes for the citizens in Orangeburg.

Mr. Pearson was a past president of the Rotary Club. In 1955, he received the Fuller Award for the entire United States from the American Waterworks Association. He was president of the Home Building and Loan Association for almost twenty-five years.

Mr. Pearson was very active at St. Paul's Methodist Church. In his retirement, he served as supervisor of church properties.

He married the former Virginia Claire Davis, and they had two daughters: Doris P. Patrick and Elma P. Owens. After his wife's death, he married Lorena Lowe. He died in 1968.

WALTER M. RIGGS (1873–1924)

Walter Riggs left an indelible mark on Clemson University. As a young professor in 1896, he helped establish the first football team there. Because of the newness of this sport, he had to be the coach also, as no one else was familiar with this upcoming sport. From 1909 until his death in 1924, he was the beloved president of Clemson.

Born in Orangeburg in 1873 to Harpin and Emma Gowan Riggs, he received his early education there. Walter Riggs obtained his bachelor's degree from Alabama Polytechnic Institute (now known as Auburn University) in 1893 and a master's degree in engineering there in 1894. He was not only the first honor graduate of his class, but he was an athletic star as well. Riggs was the captain and catcher on the baseball team and a star on the football team. After teaching for two years there, he came to Clemson to teach mechanical and electrical engineering.

Courtesy Orangeburg County Historical Society.

Professor Riggs organized the first Clemson football team in 1896 and served as its coach for two of the first four years. As he needed more time for his teaching duties, he convinced the president to hire his former coach at Auburn to take over. This man was none other than John Heisman, for whom the famous Heisman Trophy is now named. This honor is awarded to the nation's most outstanding college player each year.

Mr. Riggs also organized the Clemson Glee Club. He established the South Carolina Intercollegiate Athletic Association in 1900 and served as its president for many years. He also served as the vice-president and president of the Southern Intercollegiate Athletic Association.

In 1909, Walter M. Riggs was chosen as the acting president of Clemson College. In 1911, he was selected as president, in which position he served until his unexpected death at an educational meeting in Washington, D.C., in 1924. As president, he created new efficiencies in the college's operations as well as introduced architectural studies and enlarged the extension program. Enrollment doubled during his administration, and Clemson was acknowledged as one of the leading land grant colleges in the country.

Because of his outstanding leadership in athletics, the new football field in 1915 was named Riggs Field. Today, this field is home to Clemson's soccer team.

Mr. Riggs married the former Marie Louise Moore from Auburn, Alabama, in 1897.

Alexander S. Salley (1871–1961)

As South Carolina's official state historian for forty-four years, Alex Salley was a legend in collecting and compiling our state's history during his tenure.

Mr. Salley was born in Orangeburg County to Alexander McQueen and Sallie M. Salley. He graduated from The Citadel in 1892. Afterward, he read law in Charleston and was admitted to the bar in 1899, although he never practiced law after that. While in Charleston, he became the secretary treasurer of the South Carolina Historical Society. His organizational skills not only put the society on sound footing but also produced a fivefold increase in membership. While working for the local paper, the *News and Courier*, as a statehouse reporter, he was called in to the capitol to assess a newly found room full of old documents that just happened to be records from the Revolutionary War era. In 1905, the legislature created the job of secretary of the then functionless State Historical Commission. Mr. Salley was the obvious choice and thus began his career as South Carolina's state historian, and the commission thrived under his leadership.

Through his efforts, several important documents were rediscovered during his tenure. One was the first constitution of the state of South Carolina

ALEXANDER S. SALLEY, JR.

Courtesy Yates Snowden, History of South Carolina.

from March 26, 1776. This was the first state constitution of any of the original thirteen states. Another priceless find was a copy of the Bill of Rights sent to South Carolina to approve as amendments to the United States Constitution. Only ten of these are known to still be in existence.

Mr. Salley collected many precious documents and museum articles through the years. He has published over seventy-five volumes for the State Historical Commission and at least twenty more for other agencies on various aspects of South Carolina history. Because of his tremendous talents in preserving our state's history, the state law that mandated retirement at age seventy-two was extended three times in his case, with special legislation to allow him to continue these valuable services until he was seventy-eight years old.

Alex Salley married the former Harriett G. Milledge from Georgia in 1918. She was a direct descendant of a former governor as well as a U.S. senator from Georgia.

Mr. Salley was a South Carolina legend because of what he did to preserve our state's rich history during his lifetime.

MARION SALLEY (1885–1937)

Miss Marion Salley has been one of Orangeburg's premier historians through the years. Her numerous articles about life in Orangeburg have been a treasure-trove of information for researchers.

Marion Salley was born in 1885 in Orangeburg to Sheriff Alexander McQueen Salley and Sallie M. Salley. She attended the local schools and graduated from Winthrop College.

Courtesy Gene Atkinson Collection.

As a historian, she was deeply interested in preserving the history of the Orangeburg area. As a correspondent for several newspapers, she authored many articles about life in Orangeburg in the 1700s and 1800s. After her death, many of these writings were published as a collection in a book made available by the Orangeburg County Historical Society. Her brother, Alex S. Salley, was South Carolina's official state historian for forty-four years.

Miss Salley was a faculty member of Orangeburg High School for a number of years. She was a charter member and past president of the local chapter of the Winthrop Daughters, a local benevolent association. Additionally, she served as vice-president of the Winthrop College Alumnae Association. As a member of the United Daughters of the Confederacy, she served as president of the local chapter as well as being the state president. Later, she was elevated to the national office of historian general.

Marion Salley was commended for her work in providing proper information for textbooks in our state schools. She also won numerous awards for her essays through the years.

Miss Salley was very active at St. Paul's Methodist Church. She never married and died in 1937 after an illness of several months.

Dr. Raymond R. Salley (1898–1971)

Dr. Raymond R. Salley was a prominent Orangeburg citizen who practiced veterinary medicine for fifty-two years.

Dr. Salley was born in Salley, South Carolina, in 1898 to Dempsey Henry and Carrie Tyler Salley. He attended the public schools there and graduated from the Auburn School of Veterinary Medicine in 1919. He served as the Orangeburg County veterinarian for nine years. Dr. Salley was

Courtesy Everette Salley.

very active in his profession and served on the state association's board of directors as well as several committees. He was the state president in 1926 as well as a director and president of the Southern Veterinary Association.

Locally, Dr. Salley served on the board of trustees of the Orangeburg City Schools for eighteen years, four of them as chairman. Fraternally, he was a member of the Masonic order and the past master of the blue lodge, as well as being a Shriner. Civically, he was a member of the Rotary Club for many years.

Dr. Salley was a veteran of World War I and served on the town council in Salley before moving to Orangeburg. He was a member of the board of directors of Home Building and Loan Association and served as its vice-president for many years.

Dr. Salley was a devout member of First Baptist Church, where he served as a trustee and a deacon.

He married the former Reba Sheppard, and they had two children: Dr. W. Everette Salley and Anna Louise S. Inabinet. Dr. Salley died in 1971 after serving the veterinary needs of our area for fifty-two years.

CHIEF T. ELLIOTT SALLEY (1892–1957)

T. Elliott Salley served with distinction as Orangeburg's police chief from 1942 to 1956. He was highly respected by both the community and the officers on his force.

Mr. Salley was born in 1892 to Julian Alexander and Lizzie Bull Salley. He was educated in the Orangeburg City Schools and The Citadel and graduated from Davidson College. During World War I, he served overseas in France and was twice wounded in action.

Upon his return from the war, he became the deputy clerk of court in Orangeburg. Later, Mr. Salley was a bookkeeper with the Bank of Orangeburg and its successor, the Orangeburg National Bank. In 1924, he organized his own business, the Salley Supply Co., and subsequently established a construction business. Mr. Salley became the magistrate in 1940 and was appointed as Orangeburg's chief of police in 1942, in which position he served until 1956. He was an honor graduate of the FBI National Academy in 1946.

Courtesy Salley Johnson.

Chief Salley served as president of the South Carolina Law Enforcement Officers Association and the FBI National Academy Associates of South Carolina.

Mr. Salley's civic service was exemplary, as he served as president of the Orangeburg Chamber of Commerce, commander of the local Masonic lodge, commander of the American Legion and commander of the VFW. He was also a past president of the Forty and Eight.

Mr. Salley was a devout member of First Presbyterian Church, where he served as an elder.

Chief Salley married the former Hattie Brunson, and they had two daughters: Elizabeth S. Presson and Harriett S. Slade. He died in 1957 after an extended illness.

Henry R. Sims (1893–1966)

Attorney, newspaper editor, state senator, Winthrop College president and businessman, Henry Sims has been a committed public servant throughout his life.

Courtesy Edward Sims.

Mr. Sims was born in 1893 to James Loyal and Georgia Sheridan Sims in Orangeburg. He graduated from Orangeburg High School and then Wofford College in 1913.

Mr. Sims and his twin brother, Hugo, were attorneys together from 1916 to 1944, and they were co-editors of *The Times and Democrat* from 1913 to 1936. They were also the city attorneys and counsel to Southern National Bank.

Henry Sims was a board member of Sims Publishing Co. and Orangeburg Theatres, Inc. He was a member of the South Carolina House of Representatives from 1923 to 1925 and the Senate from 1930 to 1944. As chairman of the Senate Social Security Committee, he was responsible for the creation of the South Carolina Unemployment Compensation Act of 1936 and the Public Welfare Act of 1937.

Vitally interested in education, he was selected to be president of Winthrop College in Rock Hill in 1944, a position he held until his retirement in 1959. He was admired for his administrative talents while leading Winthrop.

Mr. Sims served as president of the South Carolina Conference for Social Work in 1945. Fraternally, he was a Mason and an Elk.

Henry Sims was deeply interested in history and was a member of several state and regional historical associations.

He married the former Letitia Key in 1918. Mr. Sims died in 1966. He was considered to be a man of deep thought and abundant energy in life's pursuits.

HUGO S. SIMS SR. (1893–1951)

Hugo Sims Sr. was a man of great influence on the educational, journalistic and business world of South Carolina. As a member of the local school board and as editor of *The Times and Democrat*, he cast a giant shadow on the life of Orangeburg.

Courtesy Ginger Risher.

Hugo Sims Sr. was born in 1893 to James Loyal and Georgia Sheridan Sims. He received his education in the Orangeburg City Schools and Wofford College, where he graduated in 1913. Afterward, he studied law in the office of Raysor and Summers and then established a law firm with his twin brother, Henry. Mr. Sims was the city attorney for Orangeburg from 1921 until his sudden death in 1951. He also served as the county attorney, counsel for the city schools and counsel for Southern National Bank.

At the family-owned newspapers, he served as the editor of both the *Orangeburg Sun* and *The Times and Democrat.* In 1917, he founded and was the editor of Editor's Copy, a national newspaper syndicate that served more than five hundred newspapers across the United States and Canada.

Mr. Sims was deeply interested in education and served with distinction on several boards. Among these were the Orangeburg City Schools, where he served from 1933 to 1945, Claflin College and the joint board for both Columbia College and Wofford College. After the latter two separated their boards, he became the chairman of the board of trustees at Wofford College until his death in 1951.

He continued his educational guidance at St. Paul's Methodist Church, where he taught the Young People's Sunday School Class for thirty-five years.

Hugo Sims married the former Lucile Howell from Orangeburg, and they had three sons: Hugo Jr., Henry II and Edward. Mr. Sims died in a tragic car accident in 1951 at the height of his career. Coincidentally, he was returning from a board of trustees meeting at Wofford College that he had chaired when the accident occurred.

JOHN WILLIAM "J.W." SMOAK (1867–1951)

Growing up as a boy with little opportunity for school but an ambitious heart and work ethic, J.W. Smoak became an Orangeburg icon in the business world. His J.W. Smoak Hardware Co. was one of the flagship businesses in downtown Orangeburg for many years.

Mr. Smoak was born in 1867 in Perry, Georgia, to John W. and Lavinia Ayers Smoak. J.W. Smoak's father died before he was one year old, so his mother returned with him to her home in Orangeburg County. As a young man, he attended Eastman's Business College in Poughkeepsie, New York. When he was fifteen years old, he went to work for Mr. George Cornelson, one of Orangeburg's leading businessmen of the time, at his general merchandise store. After ten years of learning the merchandising business there, he set up his own business in 1892 with Daniel Marchant, operating a shoe store.

In 1895, he founded the J.W. Smoak Hardware Co., and the rest was history. His business sold everything from hardware to milling supplies, heating stoves to farm implements. Through his hard work and perseverance, this business flourished and became one of Orangeburg's leading mercantile enterprises. Mr. Smoak was always a leader in many Orangeburg endeavors, such as the annual Fall Festival (a precursor of the Orangeburg County Fair), carnivals, bazaars and parades. He was also a member of the Elliott Independent Hook and Ladder Co., one of Orangeburg's volunteer fire departments.

Courtesy Merle Cox.

Mr. Smoak loved baseball and was a very adept player at shortstop for the Orangeburg Diamonds, a local all-star team that played against neighboring towns. During his early days when he was eighteen years old, he was the best player by far on the team.

When the Orangeburg County Fair Association was formed in 1911, he was elected president later that first year, and he held that position for forty years until his death in 1951. Mr. Smoak also served on the Orangeburg County Highway Commission for twelve years as well as being its chairman. In the financial world, he was a director of the Edisto National Bank. Mr. Smoak also operated a large farm for thirty-five years. He was a charter member of the Rotary Club and was a member of the Masons, the Elks and the Knights of Pythias.

Mr. Smoak was a stalwart member of St. Paul's Methodist Church and served on the board of trustees for many years.

He married the former Lillie Dukes, the daughter of Sheriff and Mrs. John Dukes, and they had three daughters: Merle S. Bethea, Ora S. Pratt and Angie Pearl S. Culler. He died in 1951 after a long and illustrious career as one of Orangeburg's leading businessmen.

Perry M. Smoak (1869–1940)

Perry M. Smoak was one of Orangeburg's leading businessmen during the first half of the twentieth century.

Mr. Smoak was born in the Cordova area in 1869 to Andrew James and Ann Bair Smoak. He was educated in Orangeburg.

Courtesy Yates Snowden, History of South Carolina.

Mr. Smoak began his business career in Orangeburg as a clerk in a general store. After that, he became the manager of the shoe department at the large mercantile business of George H. Cornelson. In 1898, he entered the wholesale grocery business of Jennings and Smoak with Robert Jennings. With his organizational skills, this partnership opened up several more business enterprises in the ensuing years. Among these were the Orangeburg Fertilizer Works, the Orangeburg Ice and Fuel Co., the Orangeburg Coca-Cola

Bottling Co.(along with two other partners), the Orangeburg Packing Co. and the Palmetto Baking Co. Mr. Smoak also ran a two-thousand-acre farm near Cordova. Additionally, he served as a director of the Edisto National Bank.

Civically, Mr. Smoak was a Royal Arch Mason and a member of the Elks Club. At First Baptist Church, he served as a deacon.

Mr. Smoak married the former Gertrude Boliver, and they had four children, two of whom survived to adulthood: Dorothy Smoak Brown and Perry M. Smoak Jr.

After a successful life in the business world around Orangeburg, Mr. Smoak died in 1940.

J. WEST SUMMERS SR. (1895–1939)

J. West Summers Sr. was an energetic civic and business leader in Orangeburg.

West Summers was born in 1895 in Orangeburg to Abram West and Caroline Moss Summers. He attended the Orangeburg City Schools in his formative years. For college, he attended Wofford for three years and graduated from Trinity College (now Duke University) in 1915.

Mr. Summers was quite a civic leader in Orangeburg. As president of the Young Men's Business League in 1927, now the Chamber of Commerce, he devoted a significant amount of energy encouraging city council to establish a new city hall and municipal auditorium as well as a public garden along the Edisto River. He was successful in both endeavors, and Stevenson Auditorium today is Orangeburg's beautiful downtown auditorium for concerts and other presentations. Edisto Gardens became a horticultural splendor that has been recognized as one of the finest public gardens in the Southeast.

Courtesy J. West Summers Jr.

In 1927, Mr. Summers and his brother, Carroll Summers, began developing a new residential neighborhood for Orangeburg called Moss Heights. It encompassed their grandparents' former farm that was located between what is now Broughton Street and Columbia Road. This development was the first planned subdivision in Orangeburg and was professionally laid out. Included within it were three parks. Two large granite entrance pillars were built at the corner of Broughton and Park Streets. Many fine homes were built in this substantial neighborhood.

Mr. Summers was prominently involved in the real estate and insurance businesses as well as being an officer and founder of the Orangeburg Building and Loan Association. He also served on the board of trustees of the Orangeburg City Schools.

West Summers married the former Claudia Mewborne, and they had three children: Claudia Ann S. Jenkins, Susan S. Masachi and J. West Summers Jr. He died in 1939. Mr. Summers truly loved Orangeburg, as was exhibited by his tremendous drive and energy in all his civic endeavors.

Albert J. Thackston (1869–1953)

A.J. "Cap" Thackston was the legendary superintendent for the Orangeburg public schools for forty-nine years. He literally touched the lives of thousands of students, preparing them for the future.

Cap Thackston was born in 1869 in Laurens County to Elijah R. and Anna B. Thackston. He attended the Anderson schools and Reidville Academy. After his graduation from Furman University, he began his education career in Springfield, South Carolina, and then at the Orangeburg Collegiate Institute. In 1897, he became the superintendent for the Orangeburg City Schools. At that time, the public schools consisted of ten grades, and all three hundred students were housed in one building on Sellers Avenue. There were only nine teachers, and Dr. Thackston, as superintendent, had to teach both the ninth and tenth grades himself. As Orangeburg's population grew, a new "graded school" was built on Ellis Avenue. The only athletics in the early days were calisthenics and games at recess.

By the time Dr. Thackston retired in 1946 after forty-nine years at the helm as Orangeburg's superintendent, several new facilities had been built to accommodate the growing student population. Athletics, school buses and school lunchrooms were all introduced during his tenure.

Dr. Thackston did graduate work at the University of Wisconsin and the University of Southern California and received a doctorate from Erskine

Courtesy L.P. Thackston Jr.

College. He was a member of the South Carolina State Board of Education for a number of years. For his endeavors, he received the Distinguished Public Service Award from the South Carolina American Legion.

Dr. Thackston was a member of the Rotary Club and a past master of the Shibboleth Lodge Ancient and Free Masons. For many years, he served on the board of trustees for Presbyterian College. Locally, he was a longtime elder at the First Presbyterian Church.

Cap Thackston married the former Lillian Phillips of Springfield, and they had three children: Dr. Lawrence P. Thackston, Colonel A.J. Thackston and Dorothy T. Todd. He died in 1953 after a long and distinguished career leading the Orangeburg City Schools.

DR. LAWRENCE P. THACKSTON (1899–1964)

Dr. Lawrence P. Thackston was a pioneer in the medical specialty of urology. His reputation was international, as he was asked to present papers around the world.

Dr. Lawrence Thackston was born in Orangeburg in 1899 to Albert J. and Lillian P. Thackston. He attended the public schools of Orangeburg and graduated from Clemson College in 1920. As an outstanding athlete, he played both football and baseball in both high school and college. In 1924, he received his MD degree from the Medical College of South Carolina.

During World War I, he served in the infantry, and during World War II in the medical corps.

After specializing in urology, Dr. Thackston was an integral part of Orangeburg's medical community, where he established the Urological Institute in 1937. Dr. Thackston was an acknowledged leader in the

Courtesy L.P. Thackston Jr.

medical profession and served as president of the South Carolina Medical Association, president of the southeastern section of the American Urological Association, state regent of the International College of Surgeons and a diplomate of the American Board of Urology. He also served on the board of trustees at the Medical College of South Carolina.

Fraternally, he was a Mason, an Elk, a past commander of American Legion Post 4 and a member of the Veterans of Foreign Wars.

Dr. Thackston married the former Bessie Young, and they had two children: Dr. Lawrence P. Thackston Jr. and Betty T. Baker. He died in 1964 in an automobile accident.

Lilla S. Wannamaker (1876–1940)

Lilla S. Wannamaker was the guiding spirit in establishing library services in Orangeburg.

Mrs. Wannamaker was born near Orangeburg in 1876 to Michael G. and Sophie P. Stroman. She moved to Orangeburg around age seven.

In 1896, she founded a book club, along with several other ladies, that was named the Dixie Club. She was their organizer as well as the president for the first ten years. By 1899, they had accumulated numerous books, so they started a library service for the people of Orangeburg. Her untiring efforts led to purchasing increasingly larger facilities to house the burgeoning collection of books. Mrs. Wannamaker was later very instrumental in the formation of the first public library in Orangeburg in 1936. At that time, the Dixie Club donated about twenty-five thousand books to help start the Orangeburg County Free Library. The mission statement of the Dixie Club was "to promote activities which are for the betterment of the community

Courtesy Orangeburg County Historical Society.

along educational, cultural, and spiritual lines." Some of their other community-minded endeavors included sponsoring local carnivals, the Chautauqua and the Camp for Colored Girls.

Mrs. Wannamaker took an active part in many civic endeavors in Orangeburg. Among these was serving on the board of trustees for the Orangeburg City Schools for many years. At the time, she was the only woman in South Carolina holding a position of this type.

Lilla Wannamaker was a very active member of St. Paul's Methodist Church. She also served as treasurer of the local Methodist Wesley House.

She was married to Harry C. Wannamaker, and they had one child: Harry C. Wannamaker Jr. She died in 1940 after a long career of civic service to Orangeburg.

WILLIAM WHETSTONE WANNAMAKER (1872–1945)

William W. Wannamaker was a leader in the textile industry in Orangeburg. As the owner and operator of Orange Cotton Mill, he cast a giant shadow on the textile manufacturing business.

Mr. Wannamaker was born in 1872 in Allendale to Reverend Thomas Elliott Wannamaker and Sarah Boyd Wannamaker. He graduated from the University of South Carolina in 1893, followed by the law school there in 1894. As an attorney, he was associated with the law firm of Bowman and Wannamaker. His partner, I.W. Bowman, later became a circuit judge. During the Spanish-American War, Mr. Wannamaker was an army captain and served during the Cuban occupation.

In 1905, he left the legal profession to become the sole owner of one of Orangeburg's largest cotton mills, the Orange Cotton Mill. This successful enterprise had been established in 1882 by one of Orangeburg's leading businessmen, George H. Cornelson. Mr. Wannamaker's keen leadership and organizational skills led this manufacturing concern until 1936 when his son, A.J.M. Wannamaker, assumed the helm.

Courtesy City of Orangeburg.

Mr. Wannamaker was deeply involved in several other Orangeburg businesses. He was vice-president of the Orangeburg Street Railway, a trolley car service in town, as well as a director of both the People's Bank and the Orangeburg National Bank. He was a trustee for the Orangeburg City Schools for twenty-five years. Mr. Wannamaker was elected as an alderman, now city councilman, for two terms.

Fraternally, he was a Mason and served as the grand master of Masons in South Carolina as well as the high priest for the state. For his outstanding service to Freemasonry, he received the highest Masonic award, the Albert Gallatin Mackey Medal. Additionally, he was the potentate of the Omar Shrine Temple in Orangeburg.

Mr. Wannamaker married the former Lyall Matheson, and they had four children: William W. Wannamaker Jr., A.J.M. Wannamaker, Lyall W. Lynch and Dr. T. E. Wannamaker. He died in 1945.

Miller F. Whittaker (1892–1949)

Miller F. Whittaker was the dynamic force behind the progress of South Carolina State University from 1932 to 1949. As president, he significantly

Courtesy Orangeburg County Historical Society.

raised the academic standards and the quality of the faculty and made tremendous improvements to the physical plant.

Miller Whittaker was born in Sumter in 1892 to Johnson C. and Page Whittaker. He attended the Sumter schools for eight years and then attended the Normal Department at South Carolina State and graduated from Oklahoma City High School with honors. In 1913, he graduated from Kansas State College with a BS degree as well as a master's degree in 1928. Later, he furthered his education at Cornell University and Harvard Universvty. Additionally, an LLD degree was conferred upon him by Allen University. During World War I, he served as a second lieutenant in the infantry in France.

Whittaker joined the faculty at the Colored Normal, Agricultural and Mechanical College of South Carolina, now known as South Carolina State University, in 1913 as a professor of physics. In 1925, he became head of the mechanical arts department. He was the architect and superintendent of all campus buildings for many years. As a registered architect, he designed many schools, churches and homes. In Orangeburg, the Lutheran Church and Williams Chapel AME Church were designed by him.

Professor Whittaker became the president of South Carolina State University in 1932 and served in that capacity until his death in 1949. As president, he had a vision for the college: "That each student shall give evidence of high moral character and personal worth, serious intellectual effort, and an understanding of his obligation to society. Things of the spirit, the common virtues of courtesy, honesty, integrity, and tolerance are just as important as the training of the intellect." Under his leadership, the academic standards were significantly improved, and Class A accreditation by the Southern Association of Colleges and Secondary

Schools was achieved. The quality of the faculty was also raised by the hiring of more professors with PhDs. A graduate school was started in 1946, and a law school was established in 1947. Student enrollment increased substantially, and many new buildings were constructed during his tenure.

He was a member of Williams Chapel AME Church and was a thirty-second-degree Mason.

President Whittaker never married. He died in 1949 during his presidency, and thousands passed his funeral bier out of respect for such a dynamic leader.

Marion Birnie Wilkinson (1870–1956)

Marion Birnie Wilkinson dedicated her entire life to others. She was the founder of the Sunlight Club, which conducted many community activities, as well as the founder of St. Paul's Episcopal Church. She was the statewide leader of the South Carolina Federation of Colored Women's Clubs, and at South Carolina State University, she was so close to the students that she was affectionately called "Mother Wilkinson."

Courtesy Gerry Zimmerman.

Marion Birnie Wilkinson was born in Charleston in 1870 to Richard and Anna Frost Birnie. She received her education at the Avery Institute there, where she graduated with high honors.

Mrs. Wilkinson's civic endeavors were unparalleled. In 1909, she established the Sunlight Club and was its president for many years. Under her leadership, this benevolent organization established a community center on Treadwell Street, the formation of a WPA School for Adults, the operation of a nursery school and many children's programs. She was the founder of the South Carolina Federation of Colored Women's Clubs, as well as its president for many years. Through her leadership, the Fairwold Home for delinquent girls in South Carolina was established. This later would evolve into an orphanage in Cayce that was appropriately named the Marion Birnie Wilkinson Orphanage.

During World War I, she was responsible for organizing a recreation center for African American soldiers at Fort Jackson, as well as a day room in Orangeburg during World War II. Mrs. Wilkinson was responsible for establishing the first Rosenwald School in South Carolina, the Great Branch Community School.

She was a tireless worker for the Red Cross and the Tuberculosis Association. Mrs. Wilkinson also served as a member of the board of trustees for Voorhees Junior College, as well as a member of the Interracial Commission of South Carolina.

As the "first lady" of South Carolina State University during her husband's presidency there, she spent much of her time with many student activities and organizations. She founded the YWCA on campus and raised the support to construct the "Y-Hut," which was appropriately named for her. After President Wilkinson's death in 1932, she continued to serve the college family by being in charge of the boarding department well into her eighties.

Dr. and Mrs. Wilkinson founded St. Paul's Episcopal Church and held the services in their living room for the first ten years until a sanctuary could be built.

Marion Wilkinson was married to Dr. Robert S. Wilkinson, who served as South Carolina State University's president from 1911 to 1932. They had four children: Helen W. Sheffield, Dr. Robert S. Wilkinson Jr., Dr. Frost B. Wilkinson and Lula Wilkinson. She died in 1956 after a long life of dedicated service to others.

DR. ROBERT S. WILKINSON (1865–1932)

Dr. Robert Shaw Wilkinson was the much beloved president of what is now known as South Carolina State University. He served with distinction in that capacity from 1911 to 1932. He was regarded as the father of organized agricultural and vocational work for African Americans in South Carolina.

Courtesy Orangeburg County Historical Society.

Robert S. Wilkinson was born in 1865 in Charleston to Charles H. Wilkinson and Lavinia A. Robinson. His early education was obtained at Shaw Memorial School and the Avery Institute there. He received his bachelor's and master's degrees from Oberlin College in Ohio and his doctorate degree from Columbia University in New York.

After college, Dr. Wilkinson first taught Greek and Latin at Simmons College in Kentucky. When the Colored Normal, Agricultural and Mechanical College of South Carolina opened in Orangeburg in 1896, he came to teach physics and mathematics. In 1911, he became the second president of the college, a position he held until his death in 1932.

The academic programs were substantially upgraded during Dr. Wilkinson's tenure. The area of agricultural education also made significant gains. In that era, State College had several different areas of educational programs. The preparatory program was a four-year high school program, the Normal Department offered a licentiate of instruction for future teachers and the Agricultural and Mechanical College covered the rest of the college program. The physical plant was also greatly enhanced during Dr. Wilkinson's presidency.

Dr. Wilkinson enjoyed a national reputation as an educator. He served as president of the Negro Land Grant College Association of the South, chairman of the Palmetto State Teachers' Association Executive Committee and secretary of the board of trustees of Voorhees Industrial School in Denmark. He was also a director of the Mutual Savings Bank of Charleston and the Victory Savings Bank of Columbia.

Fraternally, he was a deputy grand master of the Masons, the grand master exchequer for the Negro Knights of Pythias and was a member of the Elks and the Odd Fellows.

Dr. Wilkinson and his wife founded St. Paul's Episcopal Church and used their living room for its services for the first ten years.

He married the former Marion Birnie, and they had four children: Dr. Robert S. Wilkinson Jr., Dr. Frost B. Wilkinson, Helen W. Sheffield and Lula Wilkinson. He died in 1932 as a result of pneumonia while still serving as president of South Carolina State University. As a fitting tribute for such an outstanding educator, the first African American public high school in Orangeburg in 1937 was named Wilkinson High School.

CHAPTER 3

1950–2010

Hugo Ackerman (1910–2002)

Hugo Ackerman has singularly done more for the preservation of Orangeburg's history than anyone else through the years. Researchers visiting the Alex Salley Archives today have a plethora of information, thanks to him.

Born in Cottageville, South Carolina, in 1910, Hugo Sheridan Ackerman moved to Orangeburg as a child. He was educated at Orangeburg High School and Wofford College. After college, he held several different jobs before finding his true profession as a high school teacher in 1938 in Cameron and then in 1940 in Orangeburg. In college, he was a ROTC captain but was denied a commission in World War II due to a nerve injury in his leg. Not to be rebuffed, he entered the service as an enlisted man, serving for three years in the Pacific Theatre. This same leg injury caused his leg pain at his previous jobs, where he was required to stand up most of the day. Because teaching would allow him to sit down more, this became the overwhelming factor in his career change. Otherwise, he would not have realized his true calling, which led to being Orangeburg's premier historian.

Upon his retirement from teaching in 1972, he became the Orangeburg County Historical Society's first official archivist, although he had been assimilating much of Orangeburg's history for years beforehand. Mr. Ackerman spent countless hours working every day to collect and categorize everything he could find regarding Orangeburg's rich history. He researched every local newspaper from the 1800s on, typing up summaries of all the

Courtesy Lackey's Studio.

news articles, obituaries, etc. He would then cut these into strips and paste them in the appropriate categorical files at the archives—quite a laborious task. Additional information was procured from the vast files at the Caroliniana Library at the University of South Carolina, South Carolina's repository for its state history. As a result, there are now over three thousand files at Orangeburg's Alex Salley Archives, some containing as many as 150 pages.

Hugo Ackerman also wrote a weekly historical column in *The Times and Democrat* for many years. In 1998, he was honored by the City of Orangeburg with a Resolution proclaiming it "Hugo Ackerman Day" for his arduous efforts collecting Orangeburg's history through the years.

Mr. Ackerman and his wife, Helen, had no children. Orangeburg is deeply indebted to Hugo Ackerman for his efforts to preserve our rich heritage.

H. CIREMBA AMICK (1912–2006)

Because of his financial and organizational skills, Ciremba Amick was chosen as General Dwight D. Eisenhower's finance officer for the Supreme Headquarters Allied Expeditionary Forces. As the finance office moved from London to Versailles to Frankfurt during the last year of World War II, his skills were so legendary that the office could stop in the middle of work, pack up and be on the road in thirty minutes. His secret—the office desks and equipment were bolted to the bottoms of the shipping crates.

Ciremba Amick was born in 1912 near Leesville and graduated from Newberry College in 1933. His first job was as principal of Prosperity High School. In 1934, he began his legendary banking career with the Federal

Courtesy the Amick family.

Land Bank and later the Board of Bank Control. After World War II, he joined the Federal Reserve Bank in Richmond, Virginia, being a bank examiner, bank charter administrator and troubleshooter in the government bond department.

In 1954, Mr. Amick returned to South Carolina as executive vice-president of the newly chartered Bank of Florence. He arrived in Orangeburg in 1955 with the Bank of Orangeburg, becoming its president in 1957. After the bank's name change to American Bank and Trust, he left the presidency in the 1970s to become the comptroller for the eighteen-store Belk-Hudson department store chain, where he served until he was into his eighties.

As a member of the Orangeburg Lutheran Church, he was a Sunday school teacher and head of the finance committee. In the 1980s, he became a member of St. Paul's United Methodist Church.

Ciremba Amick's civic endeavors are quite numerous. He was a director and president of the Orangeburg Chamber of Commerce; treasurer of the Industrial Development Corporation; United Way board and general chairman; president of the Lions Club; Community Concert Board treasurer; president of the Country Club; and served on the Executive Board of the South Carolina Bankers Association. In 1961, he was selected as Orangeburg's Citizen of the Year.

He was a founder, treasurer and president of Wade Hampton Academy and also president after the merger to create Orangeburg Preparatory School. Mr. Amick's memberships included being a Mason, the Elks Club, the American Legion and the VFW.

He married Henrietta Irby in 1942, and they had two children: Jane and Harold. Mr. Amick died in 2006 after a long and illustrious career in the financial world.

J. ANDREW BERRY JR. (1912–1994)

Andrew Berry will be remembered for his enthusiastic involvement in many community-minded projects to improve the quality of life in Orangeburg.

Mr. Berry was born in Orangeburg in 1912 to Joseph A. Berry and Fannie Pike Berry. He graduated from Orangeburg High School, Duke University and the University of South Carolina School of Law. In 1936, Andrew Berry was admitted to the bar, beginning a career that spanned fifty-eight years. He served in the U.S. Navy in the Pacific Theatre during World War II.

Mr. Berry was a very civic-minded person who spearheaded many endeavors in Orangeburg. He headed the Community Concert Series here as well as being one of the driving forces in the creation of the Orangeburg Arts Center and the Orangeburg League of the Arts to provide cultural and artistic opportunities for our citizens. The Horne Wetlands Park and the nature trail in Edisto Memorial Gardens bear his footprints in their establishment. When Orangeburg businessman and philanthropist Dick Horne wanted to establish a foundation to support efforts to improve the quality of life in Orangeburg, he called on his old friend Andrew Berry to set up the foundation, outline its goals and guidelines and administer its affairs. Mr. Berry is to be commended for his commitment to making all this become a reality. There are many civic and cultural improvements, as well as opportunities and scholarships for the youth of the area, because of his hard work carrying out the wishes of Dick and Millie Horne.

Courtesy Nancy Berry.

Mr. Berry was a Methodist in his religious affiliation and served as the chairman of the board of stewards for St. Paul's

Methodist Church. Later, he was a dedicated member of St. Andrew's Methodist Church.

Andrew Berry married the former Nancy Womble of Orangeburg, and they had four daughters: Barbara, Nan, Mary and Julia. He died in 1994.

Willie S. Berry (1897–1987)

Berry's on the Hill restaurant was an Orangeburg icon for many years. Its reputation as one of the finest restaurants around was due entirely to its founder, Mrs. Willie Berry. The quality and tastefulness of the food served was lauded far and wide.

Willie Berry was born in 1897 to Sheldon and Elizabeth Perreyclear Scoville. She got her start hosting wedding teas and bridge parties using three large rooms in her home on Doyle Street. Her culinary skills and gracious entertaining were the talk of the town. At the same time, she was also running the dining room at the Hotel Eutaw. During World War II, she headed up the kitchen facilities at the flight school in Orangeburg known as Hawthorne School of Aeronautics.

It was only fitting that Mrs. Berry start her own restaurant in 1946, aptly named Berry's on the Hill. It was truly located on a hill on Summers Avenue across from the hospital. The popularity and success there propelled her move to a new and larger facility in 1956 on the recently relocated four-lane thoroughfare known as Highway 301. The exposure to tourists from all along the entire eastern seaboard traveling to Florida helped get Berry's on the Hill recommended as one of

Courtesy Willie Hayden.

the finest restaurant establishments around by Duncan Hines, AAA and *Gourmet* magazine.

Willie Berry always supervised the food preparation with an adept eye, personally approving every plate leaving the kitchen, many times sending them back for "corrections." One of her favorite exhortations was, "Please don't forget the parsley!" The seasonings and flavorings Mrs. Berry insisted upon with all the foods prepared made the quality of the meals unparalleled. No matter where an Orangeburg citizen went in South Carolina, he or she would always be greeted with conversation such as, "Oh, you are from Orangeburg. That's where that fabulous restaurant is located!"

One of the much-heralded delights of children and adults alike was Willie Berry's "apple stickies." These were small biscuits with a mixture of small apple bits, brown sugar, cinnamon and butter sprinkled on top before being baked. They became her trademark.

In the 1980s, Orangeburg Calhoun Technical College's Foundation printed a cookbook of most of Mrs. Berry's recipes. It was an outstanding success that brought back memories for many longtime Orangeburg citizens. Of course, it was entitled *Please Don't Forget the Parsley*.

Willie's husband, C.C. Berry, worked in the evenings at the restaurant after his day job as postal inspector for Orangeburg, as well as on weekends. Other family members pitched in to help too. Willie Berry will always be remembered as a gracious lady whose culinary talents were unparalleled. She died at age eighty-nine in 1987.

Judge James M. Brailsford Jr. (1910–1993)

Judge Brailsford served with honor and distinction on the South Carolina Supreme Court from 1962 to 1974. One of his colleagues said, "He is a quiet man, but speaks loudly when he writes an opinion." Senator Marshall Williams was quoted as saying, "He, in my opinion, was one of the best Supreme Court judges and trial judges. On the Supreme Court, his opinions were some of the best ever written."

Judge Jimmy Brailsford was born in 1910 in Orangeburg to James M. and Bessie Bates Brailsford. He attended Orangeburg High School, being the quarterback on the football team, and later the University of South Carolina, where he was on the boxing team. In 1934, he graduated from USC's School of Law, being selected to both Phi Beta Kappa and Omicron Delta Kappa due to his scholastic and leadership abilities.

Courtesy Mimi Todd.

He started his law practice in Orangeburg with M.E. Zeigler. During World War II, he was appointed to be the attorney for the Office of Public Administration but was drafted shortly afterward when the Selective Service regulations changed to include those who were married with children. Following basic training, he was assigned to Camp Blanding and later Judge Advocate School in Michigan. Japan surrendered before he could complete school there, and he returned to Orangeburg to resume his law practice.

Mr. Brailsford was elected to South Carolina's House of Representatives in both 1938 and 1940 but declined to run in 1942 after World War II had begun. In 1946 and 1948, he was again elected to the House. In 1949, he was selected by the legislature to be judge of the First Judicial Circuit, and in 1962 he was elected to be elevated to South Carolina's Supreme Court, where he served with distinction for twelve years until his retirement.

Among his hobbies were hunting, vegetable gardening and raising show horses. He had the distinction of having his portrait painted and displayed in the Orangeburg County Court Room where he had presided for thirteen years.

Judge Brailsford was married to Louise Tomkins, and they had four children: James III, Dan, Mimi and Martha. After his wife's death, he was remarried to Joan Ward Culler. Judge Brailsford died in 1993.

A.L. "RED" BREWINGTON (1921–2009)

Red Brewington is perhaps one of the most multitalented individuals Orangeburg has ever produced. His talents include master bridge player, superb dancer and expert tour guide, not to mention heading up many civic and oversight boards as well as helping lead the Belk-Hudson department store chain in an explosive growth pattern over his forty-seven years there.

Red was born in 1921 in Orangeburg to George and Connie Brewington. At age eleven, he began his legendary career in the department store business at Belk-Hudson under the guidance of Mr. E.O. Hudson. His duties began as a Saturday all-purpose errand boy and janitorial assistant for a grand sum of $1.40 a day. By the time he retired after forty-seven years of service, he was the vice-president of a chain that had grown to twenty-two stores in four states.

During his senior year at Orangeburg High School, he was so respected that he was elected president of the National Honor Society. Because his father had died when Red was attending high school, there was no opportunity for him to pursue a college education; however, he obtained more than the equivalent of that under the tutelage of Mr. Hudson at work.

Courtesy A.L. Brewington.

In the 1940s, with World War II raging, Red Brewington felt compelled to serve his country and enlisted in the navy. He became a pilot and was assigned to patrol the South Atlantic between Brazil and Ascension Island.

Upon his return, promotions came rapidly for such a skillful and talented person, and he ultimately became the vice-president. He oversaw the growth of the Belk-Hudson chain to twenty-two stores spread over several states.

Dancing was a natural talent of Red's that

developed into one of his social outlets. He would go to studios in Columbia and New York City on his business trips to learn all the latest steps. Whether it was the cha-cha or his favorite dance, the shag, he would glide across the dance floor with the greatest of ease. Playing bridge fascinated Red, and he achieved life master status while still in his thirties. Traveling was another pursuit that took him all over the world. In fact, he conducted his own tours for friends to some of the highlights of Europe.

Civically, Mr. Brewington was on the board of the local hospital, the Regional Medical Center, for nineteen years, ultimately becoming its chairman. Serving as president of the Chamber of Commerce, a member of the Orangeburg Calhoun Technical College Foundation Board and on two banks' board of directors were all part of his commitment of service to the people of Orangeburg. Quietly and without fanfare, he committed himself to philanthropic activities promoting the well-being of many facets of Orangeburg's life.

In 2000, he was presented the Edisto Award by City Council in recognition for his many commitments to helping improve the quality of life in Orangeburg. Our city has benefitted greatly from the services of this true southern gentleman.

Alec Taylor Brown (1898–1977)

Alec T. Brown was born in 1898 in Cross Hill in Laurens County to Richard W. and Frances Bookhart Brown. He graduated from The Citadel with a degree in civil engineering in 1919 after a stint serving in World War I.

From 1919 to 1927, he served as an engineer in the South Carolina Highway Department, ultimately becoming a divisional engineer. After eleven years in private practice, he returned to the Highway Department and was the chief engineer for the Lake Greenwood hydroelectric project. Afterward, he became the resident engineer at the Santee Cooper power plant and locks project in Pinopolis, South Carolina. During World War II, he served as a naval engineer in the Seabees.

In 1946, Mr. Brown came to Orangeburg in the capacity of city engineer. The duties of city administrator were added to that in 1955. His proudest achievements in service to Orangeburg were the establishment of a natural gas system that was vital in attracting industry and the relocation of Highway 301 from Russell Street to John C. Calhoun Drive. Although the highway relocation met much public resistance from the landowners involved,

Courtesy City of Orangeburg.

the city had no choice, as the State Highway Department would have relocated it several miles away, which would deprive Orangeburg's economy from the heavy north–south tourist traffic on Highway 301.

Other accomplishments for Orangeburg by Mr. Brown include: designing and construction supervisor for the municipal ballpark, Mirmow Field; two municipal river pavilions along the Edisto River along with sand beaches; design and construction of the Peasley Street recreation center for African Americans; the widening of Amelia, Broughton and Middleton Streets; off-street parking lots so vitally needed for the downtown business area; airport runway extension along with paving and lighting; and a doubling of the Orangeburg sewer system. After his retirement, he was elected to serve on Orangeburg's City Council.

He was a past state president of both the American Society of Civil Engineers and Professional Engineers, a past president of the Rotary Club and a past president of The Citadel Alumni Association. He was also a Kiwanis member for thirty years. Mr. Brown served in various capacities at First Baptist Church.

In 1925, he married the former Dorothy Smoak from Orangeburg, and they had one daughter: Nancy Brown Davis. In 1954, his second marriage was to Carolyn Green from North Carolina.

Orangeburg truly prospered under the keen guidance and strategic mind of Alec Brown. He died in 1977 at age seventy-eight.

Thomas B. Bryant Jr. (1905–1983)

Thomas Braxton Bryant Jr. was the only son of nine children born to Thomas B. and Tallulah Ray Bryant of Orangeburg in 1905. His educational accomplishments include graduating from Orangeburg High School in 1922, Washington and Lee University and Washington and Lee Law School in 1928. "Mr. T.B." practiced law in his beloved Orangeburg for fifty-five years until his death in 1983.

Mr. Bryant was an active member of the Orangeburg County, South Carolina and American Bar Associations throughout his professional career. For most of his career, he was associated in the Bryant and Fanning law firm in town. He served from 1930 to 1932 in the South Carolina House of Representatives and from 1944 to 1952 in the South Carolina Senate. Also, he was the city recorder (municipal judge) in town for several years. A lifelong Democrat, he had the distinction of being a delegate to the 1948 Democratic National Convention in Philadelphia.

Mr. Bryant was a lifetime supporter as well as a member of the board of trustees of Connie Maxwell Children's Home in Greenwood. His interest in his alma mater continued with his service as a member of the Alumni Board of Trustees at Washington and Lee. Additionally, he served on the board of trustees of Coker College in Hartsville, South Carolina. Mr. Bryant was also a member and chairman of the South Carolina Probation, Parole, and Pardon Board for many years.

Courtesy Thomas B. Bryant III.

He was a lifelong member and leader at First Baptist Church in Orangeburg.

Perhaps his greatest asset was his love of his fellow man.

There were no strangers in his life, as he was blessed with a very outgoing personality. After just a few minutes of conversation, he would clearly establish a connection with almost anyone.

Mr. Bryant married the former Cornelia Smoak in 1935, and they had two sons: Thomas B. Bryant III and Harry S. Bryant.

THADDEUS K. BYTHEWOOD SR. (1909–1989)

T.K. Bythewood owned and operated the Bythewood Funeral Home for fifty years. He was a leader not only in that industry but was also involved significantly in civic affairs in Orangeburg.

Born in 1909 to Alton E. and Felicia Sasportas Bythewood, he received his primary and preparatory education at Claflin University. In 1928, he graduated from the Renouard Training School of Embalming in New York City. He received a bachelor's of science degree from Claflin University in 1930.

After college, Mr. Bythewood joined his father in the Bythewood Funeral Home business. This funeral home was one of the largest African American–run mortuary services in the state. He was very dedicated to his alma mater, Claflin University, where he served for forty-seven years on its board of trustees, including being chairman of the Buildings and Grounds Committee.

As a businessman, he served for seventeen years on Orangeburg's Planning Commission as well as being its chairman. Mr. Bythewood was very interested in helping youth, as he served as a voluntary assistant coach at Dunton Memorial and Wilkinson High School. He also was a leader in Orangeburg civil rights activities.

Mr. Bythewood was a charter member of the Xi Psi Chapter at Claflin and was an active member of the Epsilon Omega Chapter of Omega Psi Phi fraternity for sixty years. He was a Mason for fifty-seven years and was a past master of Edisto Lodge 39, Free and Accepted Masons, Prince Hall Affiliated. He was also a life member of the NAACP.

Religiously, Mr. Bythewood was a lifelong member of Trinity United Methodist Church, where he taught Sunday school for many years.

He married Emilie Kinloch Green, and they had two children: Thaddeus Kinloch Bythewood Jr. and Alvan Emilie Bythewood. Mr. Bythewood died in 1989 after a long and distinguished career as a mortician and civic leader in Orangeburg.

Martin C. Cheatham Jr. (1927–2001)

Since his arrival in 1966, Martin Cheatham was a dynamo of energy to make Orangeburg a better city in which to live. His contagious enthusiasm was a blessing to our fair city.

Born in Greenville in 1927 to Martin C. Cheatham and Genevieve Moore Cheatham, he was the spark plug of Greenville High's football squad even though he was only the manager of the team. After attending Furman University, he went to work for Thomas McAfee Funeral Home in Greenville. A year later, he found himself working for Southern Bell, where he quickly rose up the ladder into leadership positions.

Assigned to Orangeburg as its local Southern Bell manager, he hit the ground running, involving himself in many community endeavors. After retiring in 1978, he went to work in real estate, where he remained until his death. Through the years, several people have said that the only reason they chose to locate personally or with their business in Orangeburg was due entirely to the way they were treated by Martin Cheatham when they came to consider Orangeburg.

Courtesy the Cheatham family.

Martin Cheatham was very active in many civic activities. As a member of the Kiwanis Club, he was a past president. He was a lieutenant governor for the lower one-fourth of the state, organized a high school Key Club, founded and organized the Kiwanis Junior Golf Tournament and founded and organized the Richard Osborne Memorial Invitational Golf Tournament, where only the winners of South Carolina's junior tournaments competed to determine a champion of champions. He was also a volunteer high school golf coach.

Mr. Cheatham was a past president of the Telephone Pioneers, a member of the Orangeburg Human Relations Council to promote racial harmony in Orangeburg, chairman of the steering committee for Orangeburg's YMCA, a member of the Capital Campaign Committee to raise funds for Orangeburg's new hospital in the late 1970s and served on the board of directors of the American Red Cross. Because of his genuine service to mankind, he was selected as Orangeburg's Citizen of the Year in 1976 as well as received the Kiwanis Distinguished Service Award in 1991.

In 1989, Martin Cheatham was elected mayor of Orangeburg, in which capacity he served for eleven years until his death in 2001. As mayor, he was the driving force behind the major restoration of our municipal auditorium, Stevenson Auditorium, which was a $900,000 project. He was instrumental in planning expansions and improvements to our beautiful city-owned Edisto Memorial Gardens, where over 600,000 visitors come annually. Additionally, he played a major role in establishing the Christmas lighting displays in the gardens. Martin was also very active in establishing the Downtown Orangeburg Revitalization Association to improve the downtown business district. He established the annual Mayor's Prayer Breakfast and was a strong supporter of Project Hope, a biracial group that met regularly to promote racial harmony. The creation of a city-county industrial park was high on his agenda, too.

Mayor Cheatham had the ability to be a great diplomat who could build a consensus and bring people together. One of his greatest credits was helping bring the Caucasian and African American communities together. He was truly colorblind in racial matters. He frequently was referred to as one of the best ambassadors that Orangeburg has experienced.

In 1948, he married the former June Taylor, and they had four children: three sons, Sam, Mike and Deck, and a daughter, Harris. His second marriage was to Faye Roe. After a long and progressive tenure in Orangeburg, he died in 2001 while still in office as mayor.

WILLIAM J. CLARK (1913–1985)

Called the "Gray Fox" because of his prowess in coaching high school football, Coach Bill Clark was a coaching legend in South Carolina.

William J. Clark was born in 1913 in Union, South Carolina, to E.C. Clark Sr. and Essie Jones Clark. In high school, he was an outstanding athlete who set the state record for the 440-yard dash that stood for over thirty years. At Presbyterian College, he was on the football, track and boxing teams while receiving a BS degree in chemistry in 1934. He later received a master's degree in education at the University of South Carolina.

Courtesy Warrior yearbook.

Mr. Clark's early coaching career was served in Summerville, North Charleston and Sumter High Schools. While at Sumter, his teams went to the state championship several times.

As an army reservist, he was called to active duty during World War II and ultimately rose to the rank of lieutenant colonel on General Mark Clark's staff. After the war, he returned to coaching, first back at Sumter and then as an assistant coach at Presbyterian College. In 1948, he came highly recommended as the new head coach at Orangeburg High School, where he remained for twelve years. Coach Clark was known as a master strategist who could win by outsmarting the opposing teams. He instilled this ability into his players. At Orangeburg, his teams achieved a mark of ninety-five wins, thirty-one losses and nine ties, always having a winning season.

As an educator, he became principal of Orangeburg Junior High School (subsequently Thackston Junior High) for eight years before becoming principal of Orangeburg High in 1964. In 1965, Mr. Clark became superintendent of the Orangeburg schools, a position he held until his retirement in 1977. It was during this time that he led the Orangeburg schools through desegregation. His strong leadership skills helped make this transition smoother during these pivotal times. In 1976, Mr. Clark was honored as the South Carolina Superintendent of the Year. In 2003, he was posthumously inducted into the South Carolina Coaches Hall of Fame. The civic clubs of Orangeburg named Bill Clark as the 1968 Citizen of the Year. He served on the Orangeburg County Mental Health Commission and the local American Red Cross board, as well as the United Way board. Mr. Clark was also president of the local chapter of the American Field Service, which sponsored foreign exchange students in the area. He was a dedicated member of First Baptist Church in Orangeburg.

Mr. Clark married the former Pat Stanton, and they had two daughters: Patty and Barbara. He died in 1985 after a long and illustrious career in coaching and education.

JANE CRUM COVINGTON (B. 1921)

Rightfully so, Jane Covington has been referred to as the first lady of golf in the Carolinas. She was the domineering female golfer for over two decades in the two Carolinas.

Born in Orangeburg in 1921 to William C. and Anna "Tebie" Wannamaker Crum, her father encouraged her to take up golf as a teenager. In fact, in her senior year at Orangeburg High School, she was runner-up for the country club championship against all the men. At the University of South Carolina, she was on the men's golf team until the athletic director restricted females from participating.

Courtesy Jane Covington.

While in college, she won tournaments two years in a row on the Florida circuit at Palm Beach's Biltmore Golf Club. Later, at a match in Florida, she carried the legendary golfer Babe Zaharias to the seventeenth hole before losing.

After college, she moved to the army's Aberdeen

Proving Grounds in Maryland to teach school during World War II. Her husband, Hub Covington, became the post athletic director there as well as was a golf champion in his own right. After the war, they returned to Orangeburg, where she continued her stellar career in golf. She was one of the co-founders of the South Carolina Women's Golf Association and became its first president, as well as won its first championship in 1949. Mrs. Covington went on to win four more state titles over the next sixteen years. In 1948, she was president of the Carolinas Women's Golf Association and then went on to win its championship five times through 1966.

On a national level, she qualified to play in the 1941 U.S. Women's Amateur at the famous The Country Club in Brookline, Massachusetts. In 1955, she again participated in the U.S. Women's Amateur and advanced to the quarterfinals before losing to the eventual champion.

Mrs. Covington represented South and North Carolina in the Carolinas-Virginia Team Competitions from 1957 to 1973 and served as its captain in 1959. Additionally, she and her husband won numerous couples championships through the years. At the Country Club of Orangeburg, she won the women's club championship many times. Being ever gracious to give others a chance, she would only enter it fewer than half the years it was held.

Still displaying tremendous golfing prowess as a senior, she won the South Carolina Senior Women's Golf Association's championship six times.

Jane Covington was the recipient of numerous accolades through the years, including three halls of fame: the South Carolina Athletic Hall of Fame in 1973, the South Carolina Golf Hall of Fame in 1978 and the Carolinas Golf Hall of Fame.

She was a member of the University of South Carolina Women's Board of Visitors and the Hillcrest Recreation Commission for the city-owned golf course in Orangeburg from 1971 to 1999 as well as its first chairman.

In 1944, she married Hub Covington, and they had three children: Jane C. Jeffords, Ellen C. Warren and Bill Covington.

William B. Cox (b. 1925)

Starting on a small one-acre plot in 1954, Cox Wood Preserving Co. began from very humble beginnings. Today, Cox Industries has grown to employing over five hundred people in locations across five states. Bill Cox began the business by pressure-treating fence posts to resist rotting. Now, there are myriad wood products produced for many different applications.

Bill Cox was born in Charleston, South Carolina, to Burket and Mahaley Cox in 1925. His early education was at Wando and Moncks Corner, South Carolina. After high school, he served in the U.S. Army as a paratrooper from 1944 to 1946. While in the Pacific Theatre in World War II, he was among the first ground troops to serve in Japan. After the war, he attended The Citadel for two years on the GI Bill. Mr. Cox then began his working career doing bridge construction for the South Carolina Highway Department's engineering division.

In 1950, he went to work for his father-in-law in Columbia in the wood-preserving business, which was a new innovation at the time. Subsequently, he started Cox Wood Preserving Co. in Orangeburg in 1954. His business was truly a small-town success story, growing from one acre to over thirty-five acres and over 250 employees in Orangeburg alone. From a $200 a week payroll in the beginning, Cox Industries today produces over $150 million in yearly sales.

Because of Bill Cox's energetic success, he was named South Carolina Businessman of the Year in 1983. He is a past president of the South Carolina Wood Preserving Association, past president of the Quality Wood Preservers' Society and a director of the American Wood Preservers' Association. Locally, he has served on the board of directors of First National Bank, now South Carolina Bank and Trust.

Courtesy William B. Cox.

Bill Cox has been a faithful member of First Baptist Church in Orangeburg, as well as serving as a trustee. He was named a Paul Harris Fellow by the Rotary Club of Orangeburg, only one of two nonmembers ever to receive that honor.

In 1947, he married Catherine Powell, and they had four children: Bill Jr., Cathy, Bob and Vickie.

Orangeburg is blessed to have Bill Cox as such a productive community businessman. His influence on our city's success is immeasurable.

Austin Cunningham Jr. (1914–2009)

If there ever was a true advocate for Orangeburg, Austin Cunningham would certainly top the list. His personal career was an amazing success story, but his energy level for Orangeburg was full throttle.

Austin Cunningham was born in Washington, D.C., in 1914 to Austin and Clotilde Cunningham. After his father died when Austin was a child, he entered the workforce as one of four pages at the U.S. Supreme Court at age fourteen and served there for four years. William Howard Taft was presiding as chief justice, and Oliver Wendell Holmes was the senior associate justice at the time. The justices had no personal offices at that time and had to work out of their homes. The pages delivered briefs and transcripts on some of the most sensitive of cases by way of ordinary streetcars. Austin would attend night school to finish his high school education as well as college later. For several years, he worked at the FBI in the inner sanctum office of J. Edgar Hoover, the legendary director. He graduated from law school in 1940 and later studied at Harvard University, the University of Chicago and Oxford University. During World War II, he served in the Army Air Corps.

Courtesy Austin Cunningham.

Early in his career, he worked for the Thomas Edison Co. Ultimately, he headed up five different companies as well as stints at Magnavox and Sunbeam.

He located in Orangeburg in 1974 when he directed the operations of two Sunbeam plants, one in Manning and the other in Denmark. After retiring, he owned several fast-food restaurants here. His greatest service to Orangeburg came in his many community endeavors.

As a patron of the arts, he established the South Carolina Philharmonic Orchestra concert series in town. In 1984, he was invited to the White House to be honored by President Reagan for the very successful Economic Recovery Program he chaired that provided summer jobs for 264 area youth. Mr. Cunningham was very involved with the Chamber of Commerce, the Community of Character program, the new hospital's major gifts program and the People's Assault on Drugs and was progenitor of the Elder Hop on New Year's Day to provide funds for the Meals on Wheels program for the Council on Aging.

As a writer, he wrote weekly columns for *The Times and Democrat* with his cerebral and philosophical thoughts. In fact, at age ninety-four, just three weeks before his death, he wrote his last column from his hospital bed.

Mr. Cunningham's honors are many. He received the Order of the Palmetto, the Orangeburg Citizen of the Year award in 1998, the Most Distinguished Elder Citizen of the Year in South Carolina in 1988 and the Distinguished Service Award at South Carolina State University in 1995.

In 1946, he married his wife, Jacqueline, and they had three children: Katherine Janus, Amy Cunningham and Austin Cunningham III. After his death in 2009, Mr. Cunningham was lauded as a whirlwind of energy who made Orangeburg a better place in which to live.

JULIAN HUBERT DEAN (1915–2000)

Julian Hubert Dean was born in Ninety Six, South Carolina, in 1915 to James and Elizabeth Dean. He was the youngest of seven children. He came to Orangeburg in the 1930s, where he graduated from South Carolina State's College Preparatory School as well as with a BS in chemistry in 1937. While there, he received the Jack Bryant Award for the highest grade average in chemistry.

After college, he went to work for the T.E. Wannamaker Chemical Co. In the 1950s, this facility became known as Ethyl Chemical Co. in Orangeburg. He was the first African American chemist to be employed in a chemical facility in South Carolina. With only a brief interlude, he was employed there for forty-three years. Mr. Dean's positions included being a chemist, area superintendent, research and development chemist and in technical services. During that time, he helped place hundreds of students from Claflin University and SC State University in part-time student jobs as well as permanent placement afterward.

Courtesy *Juliette Satterwhite*.

Through the years, Mr. Dean has received many awards and honors. Among these are: 1981 Alumnus of the Year for the Orangeburg Chapter of SC State's Alumni Association, 1981 Kappa Man of the Year by the Orangeburg chapter of Kappa Alpha Psi, 1983 Distinguished Alumnus Award at SC State and grand marshal for SC State's Homecoming parade in both 1984 and 1995.

He was a loyal member of New Mount Zion Baptist Church, where he served on the trustee board for many years and was chairman of the building committee.

In 1942, he married Amanda Georgiana Roundtree, and they had two daughters: Evelyn Dean Guilford, EdD, and Juliette Dean Satterwhite, RN. He died in 2000, just two days after the death of his wife, after fifty-eight years of matrimony.

Earl A. Dukes (1917–1994)

Orangeburg has been well known for its barbecue restaurants for some time, and Earl Dukes stands out as an icon in that field.

Earl Dukes was born in 1917 in the Canaan community near Orangeburg to Manuel Victor and Ethel Bonnette Dukes. His education was obtained at a one-room schoolhouse known as the "Corner School" in Canaan.

Mr. Dukes experienced several different types of employment until he found his true niche. At first he became a truck driver. After that, he operated

Courtesy Earl Dukes Jr.

a Texaco service station on Russell Street, where Orangeburg's Department of Public Utilities is located today. Next, he ran another service station that later became Silcox's station and is now Pooser's Auto Sales.

It was in 1955 that Earl found his true calling when his brother, Danny Dukes, encouraged him to enter the barbecue business. His first restaurant was at the corner of Columbia Road and Chestnut Street, about where Kentucky Fried Chicken is now located. Shortly afterward, he relocated to Whitman Street, where he earned his fame as the barbecue king. After twelve years, he sold this thriving business and established his next barbecue restaurant in Cameron, South Carolina, in the old firehouse. In 1984, he relocated back to Orangeburg in an old horse barn on the Charleston Highway. In 1985, Earl retired after turning the business over to his son Earl Jr. and his wife, Jo Ann.

Earl Dukes was known for his outgoing, friendly personality. He was also a very Christian-oriented person and was involved with the founding of several Baptist churches in the area. Whenever there was a death in town, Earl was always there bringing food to the mourning family.

Mr. Dukes married the former Marjorie Williams, and they had two sons, Earl Jr. and Sidney, and two daughters, Gail and Pamela. He died in 1994 after being acclaimed as the man who put Orangeburg barbecue on the map.

William R. Dukes (1908–2002)

William R. "Bill" Dukes was considered to be one of the top football officials in the country. Well respected for his outstanding ability, he was selected as the head referee for the 1952 Sugar Bowl game between Tennessee and Maryland, which decided the national college football championship that year.

Born in 1908 in Orangeburg to Charlie and Eunice S. Dukes, he attended the city schools here. As the star athlete at Orangeburg High School, he was the captain of both the football and baseball teams his senior year. He rushed for over one thousand yards for each of the three years he was on the football team. In 1928, he was the captain of the University of South Carolina's freshman football team. As a married student, he left college in 1929 to enter the workforce and support his family.

Mr. Dukes entered officiating entirely by accident in 1929 when the head linesman for an Orangeburg High School game arrived intoxicated. The head coach asked Bill to come out of the stands to officiate. In 1930, he officially started his career as an official at junior varsity games and progressed up the ladder to larger high school games, small college games and large college junior varsity games. In 1940, he was asked to join the Southeastern Conference Football Officials Association, where he became well known for his fairness and game control ability. About 1940, he helped organize the South Carolina High School Football Officials Association to form a centralized system for officials and to establish standards for officials, as well as a rating system.

Courtesy Tripp Dukes.

In 1951, Mr. Dukes was unanimously selected as the president of the Southern

Conference Football Officials Association. Also that year, he was chosen as a referee for the All Marine Football Championship between Camp Pendleton, California, and Parris Island, South Carolina. His leadership and game-controlling ability were clearly exhibited when he warned the all-white Parris Island team to stop its racial slurs and profanity toward its integrated opponents. After his warning, the game resumed without any further incident.

In 1953, he joined the officials' association of the newly formed Atlantic Coast Conference, where he remained until his retirement in 1959. He was the head referee for the first ACC televised game of the week in 1954 and commented that television timeouts would give unfair advantage to the weakening team. In 1957, Mr. Dukes had the privilege of refereeing the Maryland versus North Carolina game that was attended by Queen Elizabeth II and Prince Philip, which was their first football game in the United States.

In retirement, Mr. Dukes wrote a well-praised weekly historical column about Orangeburg in the local newspaper, *The Times and Democrat.*

He married his wife, Virginia, in 1928, and they had three children: Virginia, Bill Jr. (an athletic Hall of Fame honoree at Newberry College) and Gene. He died in 2002.

WILLIAM W. DUKES JR. (1917–1998)

As an outstanding industrialist, Bill Dukes was a world leader in the propane-air industry for peak energy shaving plant technology.

Born in 1917 in Orangeburg to William Walter and Ethel Chambers Dukes, he graduated from Orangeburg High School in 1934. He graduated first in his class in electrical engineering at Clemson University in 1938. Mr. Dukes began his career as an engineer at the Charleston Navy Yard and then served as an engineer for General Electric in New England for two years before being called to active duty in World War II.

In 1946, he co-founded Applied Engineering in Orangeburg. That industry became a world leader in designing and manufacturing propane-air peak shaving plants for utility companies. It also specialized in modular systems for the chemical, petroleum and pharmaceutical industries. Applied Engineering was purchased by Daniel Construction Company in 1969 and later merged to become Fluor Daniel, a worldwide giant in the field. Bill Dukes served as vice-president and president of the Applied Engineering Division until his retirement in 1983. During his career, he authored several papers as well as

Courtesy Susan Webber.

traveled extensively in the United States and around the world as a consultant in the gas industry. Applied Engineering was the recognized world authority on natural gas peak shaving and, as a result, designed and installed over three hundred peak shaving plants here and abroad.

Bill Dukes received many industrial honors and recognitions throughout his career. He received the Distinguished Alumni Award from his alma mater, Clemson University, in 1979 as well as an honorary doctor of laws there in 1997 for his outstanding service to mankind. In 1985–86, he served as president of the Clemson University Foundation. Mr. Dukes also established the William W. Dukes Jr. Endowment for Engineering Excellence there. Locally, in 1980, he was selected as Orangeburg's Citizen of the Year and received the Kiwanis Club Distinguished Service Award in 1997.

Mr. Dukes has served on numerous boards throughout his career. Among these were First Federal Savings and Loan, First Savings Bank of Greenville, Still Hopes Episcopal Home for the Aging, Orangeburg Chamber of Commerce, American Red Cross, National Foundation of Infantile Paralysis, Orangeburg Calhoun Technical College Foundation, United Way, Regional Medical Center Foundation, Voorhees College and St. Mary's College in Raleigh, North Carolina. He was a member of the Kiwanis Club of Orangeburg for over fifty years, serving as its president and the district lieutenant governor.

As an active member of the Episcopal Church of the Redeemer, Mr. Dukes was a licensed lay reader and served on numerous committees. He was the first recipient of the President's Citation of Advancement Society of the Episcopal Diocese in 1998.

Mr. Dukes married Margaret "Peggy" Crevenston, and they had three children: Peggy, Susan and Bill.

Bill Dukes and his lifetime achievements serve as a sterling example of his service to industry and mankind.

S. CLYDE FAIR (1897–1975)

Clyde Fair was a former mayor of Orangeburg as well as a prominent business leader in the insurance and banking industry.

Mr. Fair was born in 1897 in Bowman to Samuel A. and Lillie Clyde Fair. He grew up there and later attended Orangeburg Collegiate Institute and the Carlisle Fitting School in Bamberg. Early in his business career, he was a mail carrier and banker. During World War I, he volunteered to serve in the U.S. Navy. After his return, he resumed his career in banking. After a few years of helping his father-in-law's insurance agency, he began as its full-time manager in 1925. Additionally, he managed the Home Building and Loan Association and became its secretary treasurer for forty years, starting in 1932.

Courtesy Jean Harrison.

Mr. Fair was an Orangeburg city councilman from 1945 to 1949 and was elected mayor from 1957 to 1965. His energy was behind many city improvements during his tenure. Among these were numerous street and sidewalk improvements, increased public parking areas, continual improvements to Edisto Memorial Gardens, new and improved recreational facilities for our youth and recruiting of new industrial facilities for our economy.

Additionally, from 1940 to 1960 he farmed about two hundred acres near Elloree. Mr. Fair served as chairman of the local Salvation Army Board for twenty years, commander of the American Legion, president of the Lions Club, chancellor commander of the Knights of Pythias, president of the South Carolina Municipal Association and on the board of directors of the Brookland Boys' Home.

Religiously, he was a Methodist and was a trustee and past chairman of the administrative board at St. Paul's Methodist Church. He later became a member of the First Southern Methodist Church and served on its board of stewards.

Clyde Fair was an avid traveler and extensively toured the eastern United States as well as more than twenty countries.

Mr. Fair married the former Mildred Lide, daughter of prominent Orangeburg lawyer and businessman Senator Robert Lide, and they had two daughters: Jean F. Harrison and Caroline F. Turley. He died in 1975 after an extended illness.

Clarence A. Fischer Sr. (1900–1979)

A lifelong fireman, Chief Clarence A. Fischer was a legend among South Carolina's firefighters. He is credited with establishing the standards in firefighting education and training for all of South Carolina.

Chief Fischer was born in 1900 to August S. Fischer, Orangeburg's police chief, and his wife, Elizabeth B. Fischer. In 1916, he started his legendary career as a firefighter by joining the Young America Company, one of Orangeburg's volunteer fire departments. After a brief stint working for his brother Leon in Charleston in the drugstore business, he returned to Orangeburg to work for the Morris Mirmow Department Store as a clerk. He then operated a soda fountain and cigar store in town.

But the lure of firefighting was in his blood, and he went to work with the newly established city-operated Orangeburg Fire Department in 1922. By 1928, Clarence Fischer had been made a captain, and he became assistant chief in 1932. In 1945, he became Orangeburg's second fire chief and remained so until his retirement in 1965.

Clarence Fischer studied firefighting techniques extensively at Purdue University, Oklahoma A&M College and North Carolina State University to further his firefighting education. He was South Carolina's coordinator for firefighter training for many years and established the training program

Courtesy City of Orangeburg.

for all of South Carolina's firefighters in Columbia.

Chief Fischer has been a recognized leader in several firemen's associations. He was a past president of both the South Carolina Firemen's Association and the South Carolina Fire Chief's Association, as well as an officer in the Southeastern Association of Fire Chiefs.

His keen interest in youth and athletics led him to coach and teach boxing at Orangeburg High School as well as be a trainer and assistant coach of the football team. He was a past president of the Indian Club, the booster organization for Orangeburg High. Mr. Fischer served the Kiwanis Club as its president and was a member of the board of trustees for the Elks Club here. As an active member of the Lutheran Church, he served on the church council a number of times as well as on the building committee.

Chief Fischer married the former Romie Hall, and they had one son, Al, who became a local pharmacist. Upon his retirement in 1965 as fire chief, he was highly praised by leaders in the firefighting ranks from both South and North Carolina. He died in 1979 at age seventy-nine.

SAMUEL T. FOGLE (1919–2004)

Known as "Mr. Fair," Sam Fogle dedicated his entire life to the Orangeburg County Fair.

Mr. Fogle was born in Orangeburg in 1919 to John R. and Annie Smith Fogle. He graduated from Orangeburg High School in 1936 and attended

Courtesy The Times and Democrat.

Clemson College. He left Orangeburg in 1939 and went to Washington, D.C., working as a dishwasher and busboy at a restaurant there. One day when he was clearing tables, two ladies asked him to get a cab for them. After doing so, one of the ladies tipped him twenty-five cents, and he went about his business. He later learned that the lady was former First Lady Mrs. Woodrow Wilson.

A few months later, Sam found himself in Buffalo, New York, building airplanes for the Curtiss-Wright Aircraft Company. When World War II began, he enlisted as an aviation cadet and became a maintenance pilot in Mississippi.

Sam Fogle cast a large footprint on the operation of the Orangeburg County Fair. For many years, his father was the manager of the poultry barn, and his mother was in charge of the canned goods department. He attended his first fair as a baby in a cardboard box at his mother's side in 1919. Except for during World War II, he never missed a fair until his death in 2004. Like his father, Sam also ran the poultry department for a number of years. In 1977, he became the general manager of the entire Orangeburg County Fair, serving for over twenty years. His innovative ideas propelled the local fair to be one of the best in the state.

Sam Fogle was employed for many years by DuPont at the Savannah River Site. After that, he ran a Massey Ferguson farm machinery business. Mr. Fogle also farmed at home for fifty-eight years.

Known for his sharp wit and opinionated views, his letters to the editor were constantly printed in *The Times and Democrat*, the local newspaper.

He was a member of First Baptist Church and was very involved with the American Legion.

Mr. Fogle married the former Rosie Megli, and they had two children: Jerry and Marybeth. After a long illness, he died in 2004.

REVEREND DR. W. MCLEOD FRAMPTON JR. (1908–2003)

As a Presbyterian minister for over sixty years, Reverend Dr. W. McLeod Frampton Jr. has impacted the lives of many people. But perhaps his greatest achievement was as head of the Human Relations Council in Orangeburg that followed the extreme turmoil that existed following a significant 1968 racial incident. His patient guidance as a conciliator and peacemaker played a tremendous role in reducing the tensions that existed during these strained times.

Reverend Frampton was born in 1908 in Charleston to William McLeod and Isabel Addison Frampton. He graduated from Porter Military Academy in Charleston and from Presbyterian College. He then received his religious training at Columbia Theological Seminary in Decatur, Georgia.

Over the next sixty years, he served five Presbyterian churches in South Carolina as a well as a number of churches as an interim minister after his retirement. From 1958 to 1973, he ably ministered the First Presbyterian Church in Orangeburg. One of his special loves was the famous beach retreats he conducted, where teenagers would have a week of sun and fun and, surprisingly, some meaningful worship. Years later, many of these teens, after becoming adults, proclaimed how much he had meant to them during their formative years.

Close to Dr. Frampton's heart was his love of the Kappa Alpha Order, where he served as its national president (knight commander) from 1957 to 1961. He was its national chaplain for many years until his death at age ninety-five.

Dr. Frampton can be considered the father of our state's Presbyterian Homes for retirees. His concerns for the welfare of the elderly led him to found these homes in the 1950s. He has served as president, chairman of the board and treasurer of the Presbyterian Homes through the years. One of these, Frampton Hall in Clinton, was named for him for his leadership and caring for the elderly.

Courtesy Anne Smith.

Dr. Frampton was honored by his alma mater, Presbyterian College, with the doctor of divinity degree. In 1965, he was honored as Orangeburg's Citizen of the Year for all his deeds in the community. Additionally, he was a recipient of the Order of the Palmetto from the governor's office. Dr. Frampton also was the chairman of the board of the Orangeburg County Department of Social Services for many years.

He married the former Frances Moore, and they had three children: Dr. W. McLeod Frampton III, Anne Frampton Smith and Dr. Don Frampton. He died in 2003, appropriately at the first Presbyterian Home he helped found in the 1950s in Summerville.

Dr. Robert F. Furchgott (1916–2009)

Dr. Robert Furchgott was considered to be one of the leading biomedical scientists of the world. Because of his research and discoveries, he was awarded the Nobel Prize for Medicine in 1998, one of the highest honors in the world. This was quite an accomplishment for someone who grew up in the small town of Orangeburg, South Carolina.

Courtesy Robert F. Furchgott.

Robert Furchgott was born in Charleston in 1916 to Arthur C. and Pena Sorentrue Furchgott. His early education was obtained in Charleston. His high school education was in his mother's hometown, Orangeburg, where he graduated in 1933. His classmates voted him the superlatives of "Most Popular" and "Most Handsome." Growing up, he became enamored with natural history, becoming an avid seashell collector and bird-watcher. By the time he was in high school, he knew that he wanted to be a scientist.

Dr. Furchgott received his college education at the University of South Carolina and the University of North Carolina, where he graduated in 1937. His PhD was earned at Northwestern University in Chicago. Furchgott taught and researched at Cornell University and Washington University in St. Louis before going to State University of New York Downstate Medical School in Brooklyn, New York, in 1956. He was chairman of its Pharmacology Department from 1956 to 1982 and continued his research there until age eighty-six.

Dr. Furchgott received the highest honor a scientist can receive in winning the 1998 Nobel Prize for Medicine for his discovery of the endothelial-derived relaxing factor (EDRF) in 1980 and the subsequent identification of it in 1986 as nitric oxide. According to the president of the American Heart Association, it was "one of the most important discoveries in the history of vascular medicine." Interestingly, a pharmaceutical giant picked up on one of the unusual side effects of his research and developed one of the hottest-selling drugs ever—Viagra.

Some of the research that won him the Nobel Prize was done at the Medical University of South Carolina while on sabbatical there in 1980. Because of his accomplishments, MUSC awarded him an honorary doctorate, one of several he received during his illustrious career. After his retirement at age eighty-six, he moved back to his boyhood home of Charleston and became a distinguished visiting professor at MUSC until age ninety-one.

Ever the consummate gentleman, he was a dedicated and brilliant scientist and an exceptionally gentle and humble man. In retirement, he still was an avid bird-watcher, always looking up new species he saw on his walks.

Dr. Furchgott and his wife Lenore had three daughters: Jane, Susan and Terry. He died in 2009.

Lawrence T. Garick (1917–1996)

The firm but gentle hand of Lawrence T. Garick helped shape and develop the characters and minds of many young Boy Scouts through the years. He was the legendary scoutmaster for Boy Scout Troop 45 for twenty-seven years in Orangeburg.

Mr. Garick was born in 1917 in Columbia to Arthur John and Katherine de Clemery Taylor Garick. He earned a BS in chemistry from Clemson College in 1939. While there, he was a cadet captain and company commander.

Courtesy Boy Scout Troop 45.

When World War II came about, he was called to active duty in the United States Army. He served for two years in British Guiana in South America at a lend-lease base and later served in the infantry. He was seriously wounded at the Battle of the Bulge.

Upon his return to Orangeburg after the war, Mr. Garick joined his father-in-law in the refrigeration business, where he remained for the rest of his working career. R.L.

Culler Refrigeration is now being run by the third and fourth generations of the family.

In 1947, Mr. Garick began his legendary career as a scoutmaster. As his reputation spread, many young boys joined Troop 45, and it became one of the largest troops in town. As a result, it outgrew its small scout hut, and a drive was made to secure funds to build a new and larger one. Troop 45's sponsor, the Rotary Club of Orangeburg, held many pancake and sausage suppers to do so. All of the scouts under Mr. Garick and members of the Rotary Club pitched in to help with the construction. It was occupied in 1961.

After twenty-seven years of transforming boys into well-disciplined young men, Mr. Garick retired from scouting in 1974. During his tenure, he received the Silver Beaver Award, the highest award in scouting.

Mr. Garick was a past president of the Rotary Club and a past commander of the American Legion Post 4, as well as a district commander. He served as Post 4's Chairman of Boys' State and was in charge of the Baseball Committee for American Legion baseball. He was also a member of the VFW.

Mr. Garick was an active member of the Orangeburg Lutheran Church, where he served as a Sunday school teacher and was the church treasurer for thirty-seven years.

He married the former Helen Culler, and they had two sons: Lawrence Jr. and Richard. Of course, both sons became Eagle Scouts in Troop 45. Mr. Garick died in 1996.

BETTY LANE GRAMLING (B. 1936)

Orangeburg is especially proud of Betty Lane Cherry Gramling for her many accomplishments: beauty queen, Modeling Association of America International president and longtime leader, modeling and charm school proprietor—the list goes on for this beautiful and charming resident of Orangeburg.

Born in Orangeburg to Rhude and Lurline Cherry, Betty Lane attended the public schools of Orangeburg growing up. Her college education was obtained at Columbia College, where she graduated in 1958.

She began her beauty queen winning streak as Orangeburg's Maid of Cotton and went on to win the title of South Carolina's Maid of Cotton. Later, she became the South Carolina Peach Queen, which led to the

Courtesy Betty Lane Gramling.

United States Peach Queen title. Next she won the title of Miss South Carolina Universe. Representing South Carolina at the Miss USA pageant in California, Betty Lane was first runner-up. When the queen became Miss Universe, Betty Lane became Miss USA, which allowed her to represent our country at the Miss World Pageant in London, England. When the finalists there were announced, she was crowned as Miss World; but alas, a mistake had been made, so off came the crown, and it was then correctly announced that she was actually first runner-up.

While in London, she was the guest of the Lord Mayor of London and his wife for tea. Her notoriety from the pageant led to dinner with the famous pianist Liberace and his mother and brother, as well as a tour of eight European countries, where she was warmly welcomed in each and was even called upon to present the winning trophies in various competitions.

Back in the United States, she was on the *Today Show* on television, the first of several appearances. Prior to going to London, she was offered a screen test by Howard Hughes, a contract with Bob Hope and a part in a movie, but she turned them all down to go to compete for Miss World in London. Afterward, the offers continued to pour in.

In the mid-1960s, Betty Lane established the Betty Lane School of Charm, where modeling and charm composure were taught to young hopefuls. She has been a member of the board of directors of the Modeling Association of America International for many years, as well as being its nationwide president on three occasions. Betty Lane has also been a special invitee to the

Emmy Awards as well as a gala honoring longtime actress and personality Elizabeth Taylor.

Betty Lane married Johnny Gramling in 1959, and they have four children: Cherry, Tracy, John and Lawrence.

Orangeburg is blessed to have such a beautiful and charming personality who has represented her profession in such an outstanding way.

REVEREND J.F.M. HOFFMEYER (1901–1980)

Reverend J.F.M. Hoffmeyer was truly a visionary for the future. It became a passion of his in the 1940s to establish a means of taking care of the elderly. Thus, he helped to establish the Methodist Home for the Aging in 1954, one of the first facilities of its kind to care for and nurture our older population.

Reverend Hoffmeyer was born near Darlington in 1901, the son of Herman F.L. and Lucy B. Hoffmeyer. He graduated from high school there in 1919 and from Wofford College in 1923. After that, he received his master's of theology degree in 1926 from Candler School of Theology at Emory University. He served as a Methodist minister in numerous churches

Courtesy Ed Brown.

before finding his true calling with the planning and establishment of the South Carolina Methodist Home for the Aging.

Early in his ministry, he devoted much of his energy to youth work. Reverend Hoffmeyer was very involved as a leader with youth assemblies and camps for the South Carolina Methodist Conference. He was also instrumental in guiding young men's lives through scouting.

In the late 1940s, he began his crusade to convince the South Carolina Methodist Conference to provide a caring home for the elderly. In 1953, his prayers were answered when the conference approved the purchase of 113 acres and ten buildings on the old Hawthorne flight school campus from World War II in Orangeburg to start the South Carolina Methodist Home for the Aging. Of course, Reverend Hoffmeyer was the logical choice to be the first administrator of this benevolent endeavor. This facility was one of the first of its kind and started a whole new trend that has become very prevalent today. Reverend Hoffmeyer also became a founding charter member and the secretary treasurer of the South Carolina Nursing Home Association.

The South Carolina Methodist Home for the Aging was ably administered by Reverend Hoffmeyer for its first eight years. Eventually this facility, now known as the Oaks, a United Methodist Community, grew to over one thousand acres and four hundred residents. During the early years, Reverend and Mrs. Hoffmeyer attended to every detail, even pitching in to help in the kitchen or maintenance department when help was needed. Appropriately, when the thirty-one-bed infirmary for skilled care was built in 1959, it was named the Hoffmeyer Infirmary.

Reverend Hoffmeyer married Miss Lois Folk of Holly Hill in 1926, and they had one daughter: Gerry Hoffmeyer Brown. Fittingly, Reverend Hoffmeyer spent the last months of his life in the Hoffmeyer Infirmary before his death in 1980. His footprints on the establishment of the retirement and nursing home industry will always be remembered.

Charlton B. Horger (1914–1997)

Charlton Horger was known as a distinguished attorney in Orangeburg as well as an outstanding banker.

Mr. Horger was born in 1914 to Dr. Edgar O. Horger and Inez Bowen Horger. He graduated from the University of South Carolina in 1936 and the School of Law there in 1938. During World War II, he served for three years in the Judge Advocate General Corps.

Courtesy Charlton B. Horger Family.

During his outstanding career, he served as a member of the South Carolina House of Representatives from 1946 to 1952. Mr. Horger was a member of the South Carolina Highway Commission from 1952 to 1956, serving as its chairman, and again on the commission from 1964 to 1968. He was a member of the United States Court of Appeals Judicial Conference for the Fourth Circuit. Mr. Horger served as a member of the Bar Counsel of the South Carolina State Bar and also served for two terms on the Board of Law Examiners. He was a fellow of the American College of Trial Lawyers.

Mr. Horger was an integral part of the management of First National Bank in Orangeburg for many years. He served as a director, president from 1977 to 1980 and chairman of the board from 1980 to 1987. Mr. Horger also served as a director of Home Savings and Loan Association and its successor, Home Federal Savings and Loan Association.

Charlton Horger was a dedicated member of St. Paul's United Methodist Church. He served as a teacher of the Men's Bible Class and was on the Board of Stewards.

Mr. Horger married the former Mary Catherine Rhame, and they had two children: Catherine Horger Wannamaker and Robert Rhame Horger. He died in 1997.

JESSE ELI "DICK" HORNE (1900–1970)

Dick Horne was a pioneer in the establishment of aviation in Orangeburg, not to mention his automobile dealership and many business interests.

Courtesy Dick Horne Foundation.

His impact still carries forth today with the Dick Horne Foundation, a benevolent organization that has funded many youth- and community-oriented endeavors through the years.

Jesse Eli "Dick" Horne was born in Madison, Florida, in 1900 to Aaron and Addie B. Horne. He attended the elementary and high school there and in the town of Live Oak. His dreams for a college education collapsed when his father died during his first year at the University of Florida.

Dick Horne got his start in the Ford automobile business with a part-time job in high school. In the 1920s, he became the owner of a Ford dealership in Beaufort, South Carolina. In 1931, he moved to Orangeburg and established a dealership here.

His interest in aviation began in 1921, when he first flew a Jenny biplane. Upon his arrival in Orangeburg, he helped "scrape off" a site for the city's first airport, located where Clark Middle School now exists. Mr. Horne headed the Orangeburg City-County Aviation Commission from 1937 until well into the 1960s. During this time, he was responsible for a new airport south of the city in 1937 as well as its many improvements through the years, to where it was considered to be one of the finest noncommercial airports in South Carolina.

During World War II, he was called to active duty and served as a chief pilot in the China-Burma Theatre, flying cargo planes "over the hump" in the Himalayas. He also flew in the South American and African Theatres. At the war's end, he retired with the rank of lieutenant colonel.

Back home after the war, he continued to expand his business interests by establishing Lincoln-Mercury and Ford tractor dealerships. Additionally, he built commercial buildings around town. Later, he purchased Ford automobile dealerships in Sumter, Florence and Greenville. In 1962, his dealerships accounted for 21 percent of all new Fords sold in South Carolina.

Well known for his aviation endeavors, he would fly his personal plane to Columbia or elsewhere to pick up important visitors or industrial prospects coming to Orangeburg, since the city did not have a commercial airport. Mr. Horne also gave airplane rides over the city as a graduation present for new graduates from Orangeburg High School for many years.

Mr. Horne married the former Amelia "Millie" Strakey, and they did not have any children.

Just prior to his death, he established the Dick Horne Foundation, a charitable entity that has greatly contributed to the well-being of Orangeburg through its funding of youth and community projects.

Outside of his business interests, Mr. Horne's two great hobbies were flying and golf. Unfortunately, he died in 1970 when his airplane crashed on a golf course in Florida. How coincidental that his death was connected to his two passions in life.

ROBERT E. HOWARD (1920–2009)

Robert E. "Wag" Howard was a mainstay in education in the Orangeburg schools for over fifty years.

Robert Howard was born in Georgetown in 1920 to George W. and Eliza R. Howard. He received his elementary and high school education there. In 1942, he graduated from South Carolina State University in Orangeburg with a degree in education. Later, he received a master's degree there in 1952 and an educational specialist degree from George Peabody College. Further training in the educational field was obtained at the National Academy of School Administration and Columbia University. Allen University also conferred upon him an honorary doctor of humane letters degree.

Dr. Robert Howard began his acclaimed career in education in 1942 at Wilkinson High School as a teacher and assistant coach. Shortly

Courtesy Orangeburg Consolidated School District 5.

afterward, he became head football coach as well as head coach in basketball and track. He was named assistant principal in 1943 and principal in 1955. He was especially known for instilling character and fundamentals in students' lives that would help their future success in the business and professional world.

As his career continued upward, Robert Howard was promoted to supervisory principal, assistant superintendent and associate superintendent for Orangeburg School District Five. When integration occurred, he and Superintendent W.J. Clark worked closely together to assume an orderly transition during those tension-filled years.

Professionally, he was a member of numerous educational organizations. He was president of the Orangeburg County Teachers Association, president of the South Carolina Association of Secondary School Principals from 1972 to 1974 and a member of many advisory committees to the State Department of Education.

Locally, he served on the United Way board, as president of the Edisto Federal Credit Union and on the Human Relations Committee to improve understanding and cooperation between the African American and Caucasian communities. He was also a Mason.

Fittingly, in 1991, the former Wilkinson High School facility, where he ably served for many years, was named the Robert E. Howard Middle School. After his retirement, he continued to serve the school district as its hearing officer for many years.

Robert Howard was president of the South Carolina State booster club, the Bulldog Club, as well as the "voice" of the basketball team for thirty years. He was an active member of Williams Chapel AME Church.

He married the former Mamie Williams, and they had two daughters: Bertie and Michelle. Robert Howard died in 2009.

EDWARD OSBORNE HUDSON (1905–1977)

As one of Orangeburg's most distinguished businessmen, Edward Osborne "E.O." Hudson was a giant in the mercantile field, not only in Orangeburg but in the entire Southeast. His Belk-Hudson chain of retail stores encompassed four states and twenty individual stores, three of which were in Orangeburg.

Mr. Hudson was born in 1905 in Waxhaw, North Carolina, to Thomas and Lucinda H. Hudson. He began his working career with the Belk organization at age twenty in Charlotte. Always harboring the ambition of owning his own store, he came to check out Orangeburg during the height of the Depression in 1931. He liked what he saw and established his first retail store with five employees. His determination to build a business with local employees and customer satisfaction proved to be vastly successful.

Courtesy E.O. Hudson Jr.

The Orangeburg venture proved so successful that he established a second store in Walterboro in 1936. His philosophy of providing retail stores to smaller cities and towns helped propel his Belk-Hudson chain to twenty stores at the time of his death.

Mr. Hudson was considered to be a genius in the retail industry. He was keenly insightful to his customers' needs. At the time of his death in 1977, the Belk-Hudson chain employed 690 people at the twenty stores in the chain.

Mr. and Mrs. Hudson were generous supporters of community and church endeavors. One of the special recipients of their philanthropy was Columbia College. Because of their longtime support there, one of the dormitory buildings was named Hudson Hall in 1974.

Mr. Hudson was very active at St. Paul's Methodist Church, where he served on numerous committees. He also was a member of the Lions Club.

He married the former Lillian Freeman, and they had two sons: Reverend Thomas F. Hudson and E.O. Hudson Jr. Mr. Hudson died unexpectedly on a business trip in 1977. Orangeburg will be forever grateful to Mr. Hudson for what he did for the mercantile business in the city.

James B. Hunt Jr. (1924–2004)

J.B. Hunt was widely recognized as one of the most talented high school band directors in South Carolina.

Mr. Hunt was born in 1924 in Greenville to James B. and Helena Diggs Hunt. In 1942, he graduated from Sterling High School as class salutatorian.

Music intrigued J.B. Hunt as a boy, but he was unable to financially purchase an instrument. So in the eighth grade, he bought a toy clarinet from a dime store. The school band director overheard him playing this clarinet in an amazing fashion in the boys' bathroom. The director immediately found an alto tuba for him, and by Friday night J.B. was marching with the band at halftime at the football game.

Mr. Hunt came to South Carolina State University in 1942 with a band scholarship in hand. Because he was so musically talented, he was selected to be a member of the school dance band, the Collegians, a rare opportunity for a freshman. Mr. Hunt earned a degree in mechanical engineering in 1946 and received his master's degree there in education in 1958.

J.B. Hunt was the first and only band director at Wilkinson High School, a position he held for twenty-five years. He also directed the bands at Sharperson Junior High, Belleville Middle School and Brookdale Middle School. He served as president of the state Bandmasters Association for three years and was selected as its Band Director of the Year in 1962. Upon the consolidation

Courtesy the Hunt family.

of Orangeburg and Wilkinson High Schools in 1971, he became its first band director.

During Mr. Hunt's career, he placed more than 250 students in the All State Band. He was inducted into the South Carolina State University Jazz Hall of Fame in 1987 and the South Carolina Band Directors Hall of Fame in 2001. Not only did he nurture his students' musical ability but he also instilled character in them.

Mr. Hunt was a devoted member of Mount Pisgah Baptist Church, where he served as a Sunday school teacher and deacon.

He married the former Lerlene Hilton, and they had two daughters: Deborah Hunt Woods and Dr. Marilyn Hunt Alim. Mr. Hunt died in 2004.

JARVIS BROTHERS

Orangeburg's premier family vocal musical group, the Jarvis Brothers Quintet, can truly be called a national treasure. Their singing talents that blend all vocal parts make their concerts beyond compare. The members of this a cappella group certainly can be considered Orangeburg's ambassadors of goodwill.

The Jarvis brothers were born in Orangeburg to Ulysses S. Jarvis Sr. and Anna G. Jarvis. In their formative years, they would sing with their mother accompanying them on the piano. All the brothers were active in music while attending school, either playing in the band or singing with the chorus program.

The oldest brother, Ulysses Jr., was born in 1929 and served in the United States Air Force before receiving his college degree from South Carolina

Courtesy the Jarvis Brothers.

State University in 1957. He was an educator and served as an assistant superintendent with the Dorchester schools. Reginald was born in 1935, graduated from Claflin University in 1957 and served as a teacher in the Savannah, Georgia schools. Donald was born in 1937, graduated from SC State in 1973 and was employed as a counselor and an administrator in the Orangeburg public schools. Anthony was born in 1939, received his degree from SC State in 1961 and served as an assistant principal in Orangeburg and Columbia. Born in 1945, Rogers received his college degree from SC State in 1967 and a pharmacy degree from the Medical University of South Carolina in 1976. Ulysses, Donald and Anthony also furthered their education and obtained master's degrees. Upon the death of Reginald in 2007, Donald's son, Cornell, stepped in to replace him. Cornell was born in 1959, received his high school degree from Orangeburg-Wilkinson High and is in the construction business.

The Jarvis Brothers Quintet sings mostly in the jubilee style of music. All parts are superbly blended, creating a perfect harmonious presentation.

Ulysses and Donald sing the tenor parts, Reginald and Anthony perform the baritone roles and Rogers sings bass. Upon replacing Reginald, Cornell continued singing his baritone role.

The Jarvis Brothers Quintet officially began singing as a group in 1973 and has performed at countless functions across the state and nation. Among some of the highlights were performances at the Apollo Theatre in New York and the Smithsonian Institution and the Kennedy Center for the Performing Arts in Washington, D.C.

Numerous honors and awards have been conveyed upon the Jarvis Brothers Quintet during their career. These include the Kiwanis Distinguished Service Award in 1989, the South Carolina Folk Heritage Award in 1989, the Fellowship Assemblage Award in 1990, the South Carolina State University Distinguished Service Award in 1996 and the Elizabeth O'Neill Verner Award in 2005. Additionally, they have been inducted into the South Carolina Black Hall of Fame.

The Jarvis Brothers Quintet is truly an inspiration to everyone attending their performances. Their talents are a blessing to mankind.

WILLIE JEFFRIES (B. 1937)

On the field, Willie Jeffries has been recognized as an outstanding football coach. Off the field, he is considered to be one of the most adept humorists and after-dinner speakers.

Coach Jeffries was born in 1937 to John and Irene Jeffries in Union County. He attended the public schools of Union and was salutatorian of his high school class. After that, he earned a bachelor's degree in civil engineering from South Carolina State College in 1960 as well as a master's degree later.

His coaching career began in Lancaster at Barr Street High in 1960. Next, as head coach at Granard High in Gaffney, he won three straight state championships from 1964 to 1966 and compiled a 65-7-2 record while there. Coach Jeffries began his collegiate coaching career at North Carolina A&T as the defensive coordinator. In 1973, he answered the call to be the head coach at his alma mater, South Carolina State, in Orangeburg. During his six years there, his teams compiled a 50-13-4 record and in 1976 were named national champions. Later, he became head coach at Wichita State and Howard University before returning as head coach for a second stint at South Carolina State from 1989 to 2001. His remarkable twenty-nine-year collegiate head coaching career produced a record of 179-132-6. This

Courtesy Willie Jeffries.

tremendous record included six Mid-Eastern Athletic Conference (MEAC) championships, two national titles, several postseason bowls and many coaching awards.

Coach Jeffries twice has been voted Palmetto State Coach of the Year for his successes, as well as receiving a national coach of the year award. Because of his coaching prowess, he has received many coaching offers during his stellar career.

Coach Jeffries is enshrined in four athletic halls of fame: the South Carolina Athletic Hall of Fame, the South Carolina State University Athletic Hall of Fame, the MEAC Hall of Fame and the College Football Hall of Fame. In 2002, he was honored with a lifetime achievement award from the Black Coaches Association of America. Additionally, Coach Jeffries has received both the Order of the Palmetto and the Order of the Silver Crescent awards for exemplary community service.

On the banquet circuit, he is highly sought out as an after-dinner speaker. As a master of ceremonies, his polished delivery has earned him many accolades.

Coach Jeffries married the former Mary Cauthen of Lancaster, and they had three children: Valerie, Tammy and Willie Jr.

Alan McC. Johnstone (1910–2006)

If there was one person who probably contributed the most to the industrial development of Orangeburg, Alan Johnstone would certainly fit that bill. Also, if there was one person who was a legend in propelling Orangeburg's

Department of Public Utilities into the most progressive municipal utility company in South Carolina, that too would be Alan Johnstone.

Alan Johnstone was born in Newberry in 1910 to Thomas K. and Jeanne P. Johnstone. His education was obtained in Newberry's public schools and at Clemson College, where he graduated with an electrical engineering degree in 1932. While at Clemson, he was a member of its first golf team in 1931. In 2003, as the sole surviving member of that first team, he was honored by Clemson as the honorary captain of that current golf team. Three weeks later, Clemson won the NCAA championship!

After graduation, Mr. Johnstone worked on the Buzzard's Roost hydroelectric project in Greenwood and with the United States Department of Agriculture before coming to Orangeburg in 1937 to manage the new water-softening plant. With an army reserve commission, he was called to active duty in World War II, where he served in the Pacific. Mr. Johnstone was among the first ground troops to set foot on Japanese soil after V-J Day.

Upon his army discharge in 1946, he returned to his job in Orangeburg. By 1954, he had become superintendent of both the Electrical and Water Divisions of DPU. In 1956, he became the overall general manager of DPU, where he served until his retirement in 1977. With his keen engineering and management abilities, DPU experienced an explosive growth in its volume of services during his tenure. He led DPU in entering the natural gas service in 1954. In 1971, he oversaw the transfer of the city's wastewater treatment to DPU as well as the construction of a six-million-gallon-a-day wastewater treatment plant in 1975. Mr. Johnstone was named South Carolina's Professional Engineer of the Year in 1971–72.

Courtesy Department of Public Utilities.

Industrially, Mr. Johnstone was a key member of the Orangeburg Industrial Commission, which was formed to attract industry in a post-agricultural economy in the 1950s. He served through the 1980s as well as being its chairman for fifteen years. Mr. Johnstone also served in leadership positions in the Chamber of Commerce as well as being its president.

Alan Johnstone was a devout member of the First Presbyterian Church, where he served as deacon, elder, treasurer and clerk of the session for many years, as well as being the church historian.

His allegiance to his alma mater, Clemson, was legendary. As a diehard sports fan, he never missed traveling to a home football game, with the exception of his World War II service, until age ninety-one. In 2004, he was honored by Clemson with the Distinguished Alumni Award.

In 1934, Mr. Johnstone married the former Benetta Dorrity from Newberry, and they had two children: Lilla J. Jones and Alan Johnstone. After Mrs. Johnstone's death, he married her sister, Eva. He died at age ninety-five in 2006 after a legendary life of service to the people of Orangeburg.

Frank F. Limehouse Jr. (1910–2006)

The life of Frank F. Limehouse has been filled with public service. He was on the local school board for ten years and a city councilman for twenty years, many of which were as mayor pro tem.

Born in Orangeburg in 1910 to Frank F. Limehouse Sr. and Bessie Ayers Limehouse, he was the eldest of five siblings. After attending the public schools of Orangeburg, he embarked on the train with several other local boys to go to Wofford College in Spartanburg. While at Wofford, he was the captain of the tennis team and graduated with honors in 1932. Because of the effects of the Great Depression, the only job he could find was that of an insurance adjuster and claims investigator. This was performed in Boston, Washington and Louisville, Kentucky, for about four years. In 1936, his father died suddenly, and young Frank had to return to Orangeburg to try to get the affairs of his father's business, Limehouse's Men's Store, straight in order for it to be sold. But alas, he decided to continue the business and stayed on until he retired forty years later.

Mr. Limehouse was very involved civically in Orangeburg. He was the first president of the Junior Chamber of Commerce as well as being on its board for ten years. He was a member of the Masonic order at the Equality Lodge, AFM. Mr. Limehouse was on the board of directors of the Home Building and Loan Association for several years but resigned to become one

Courtesy City of Orangeburg.

of the original members of the board of directors for First Federal Savings and Loan Association. He was very active with the Boy Scouts on both the local and state level. In the mid-1950s, Mr. Limehouse was president of the Carolinas' Retail Association.

From 1949 to 1959, Mr. Limehouse served on the board of Orangeburg School District Five. In 1959, he was elected to Orangeburg's City Council, where he served for twenty years guiding the growth of the city. During many of these years, he served as mayor pro tem. During the 1960s, his political stance for racial equality was not altogether popular, but he stood firmly for his convictions during these turbulent times.

Mr. Limehouse was an active member of St. Paul's Methodist Church and served several terms on its board of stewards.

Mr. Limehouse believed that 1939 was the most important year of his life, for that is when he met his future wife, the former Jean Mabry from Campobello. She had just graduated from college and was visiting classmates in Orangeburg when he spied her and broke in on a dance with her. True love blossomed, and they were later married. They had three children: the Very Reverend Frank F. Limehouse III, Mabry Limehouse and George Limehouse. He died in 2006 after a long and distinguished career serving the people of Orangeburg.

Dean B. Livingston (b. 1933)

In "Letters to Santa" published in *The Times and Democrat* in December 1941, eight-year-old *T and D* carrier boy Dean B. Livingston asked Santa for a small printing press. His wish was granted. The toy press, combined with his bicycle delivery route experience, helped launch an Orangeburg newspapering career that ultimately led to his becoming the *T and D*'s publisher for thirty-seven years. He retired in May 1999.

Wanting instructions on the operating of Santa's gift, the young newspaperman-to-be sought guidance from J.L. Sims, son of *T and D* publisher J. Izlar Sims. The following year, J.L. succeeded his father as the newspaper's publisher. Twenty years later, Livingston became the newspaper's publisher upon the death of J.L. Sims in 1962.

Courtesy Dean Livingston.

Born in 1933 to Alexander H. and Madge R. Livingston in North, South Carolina, his parents and their eight children moved to Orangeburg in 1940. He played football at Orangeburg High School. After the 1950 football season, Livingston was selected to the South Carolina All-State Football Team and played in the Shrine Bowl in Charlotte. He received a football scholarship to the University of South Carolina and played three years of varsity football there.

Upon graduation from USC in 1955, Mr. Livingston was commissioned a second lieutenant in the United States Air Force and served for three years as a navigator in the Military Air Transport Service. He attained more than two thousand flying hours, including flying comedian Bob Hope on his 1958 Christmas tour to entertain servicemen in North Africa, Western Europe, the United Kingdom and Iceland.

Having worked at *The Times and Democrat* during college summer breaks, he returned to Orangeburg and the *T and D* in 1959 after his military stint. He looks back on his newspaper career with satisfaction in directing the *T and D* to become the first daily newspaper in the state to convert to the new technology of offset printing, while also moving the newspaper plant from Russell Street to Broughton Street.

Mr. Livingston is a former president of the Orangeburg County Chamber of Commerce, the South Carolina Press Association and the South Carolina Press Association Foundation, and he served on many civic boards. He married the former Grace Dukes in 1955, and they had two children: Donna L. Laird and Dean B. Livingston Jr.

He is exceptionally proud of his newspaper's leadership in support of industrial development in Orangeburg, the establishment of Orangeburg Calhoun Technical College and the building of a new hospital. Mr. Livingston recalls October 10, 1972, as the "darkest day" of his life: that was the day when *The Times and Democrat*'s plant was destroyed by fire. For thirty days, the *T and D*'s editions were printed daily at the *Sumter Item* and the weekend editions at the *Rock Hill Herald*.

MASON LIVINGSTON (1921–2006)

Mason Livingston has done more than anyone else in South Carolina to nurture the American Legion baseball program through the years. Fittingly, he could be called "Mr. American Legion Baseball" for South Carolina.

Mr. Livingston was born in Livingston, South Carolina, in 1921 to Melvin K. and Pearl W. Livingston. He attended grammar school there and high school in North, South Carolina. Mason was only seven years old when his father died.

He worked at several different jobs until entering the army in March 1942 during World War II. He went ashore in France right after D-Day and saw much action at St. Lo, the Brest peninsula, Metz and the Battle of the Bulge. Of the 300 days he experienced on the European continent, 277 of them

Courtesy Annie Ruth Livingston.

were in combat time. As a result, he was awarded five Bronze Stars as well as a presidential unit citation.

In 1947, Mr. Livingston began his civil service career as a letter carrier for the United States Postal Service.

His involvement with the American Legion began in 1945. Because of his love of baseball, he began as a volunteer with its baseball program. By 1961, he had been appointed as the athletic director for American Legion Post 4, a position he held until 1970. His teams won three state championships during those years. He was also very instrumental in having Orangeburg selected as the site for the 1966 American Legion World Series. Mr. Livingston served on the state baseball committee beginning in 1974 for almost twenty-five years, as well as being the state chairman for about ten years. Locally, he was the post commander on two different occasions and served as the district commander for almost twenty years. In 1992, Mr. Livingston was honored as South Carolina's Co-Legionnaire of the Year. His devotion to the American Legion and American Legion baseball was unparalleled.

Mr. Livingston married the former Annie Ruth Dominick, and they had two sons: Marion and Al. He died in 2006 after sixty years of devotion to the American Legion.

LOIS D. LUSTY (1915–2005)

ARTHUR J. LUSTY JR. (1915–1990)

Lois and Art Lusty were the driving forces behind promoting the arts in Orangeburg. They founded the Orangeburg League of Arts and were also the genesis behind the Orangeburg Arts Council, which led to the development of the old run-down river pavilion into a beautiful showplace for promoting the arts in Orangeburg.

Lois Lusty was born in 1915 in Milwaukee, Wisconsin, to Fred and Lillian Drmolka. She graduated from Wayne State University in Detroit and later obtained a master's degree in education. Over the years, she taught kindergarten as well as being a teaching child psychologist.

In 1915, Art Lusty was born to Arthur and Rowena Lusty, also in Milwaukee. He played basketball at Wayne State University and received his degree in education there. Some of his early jobs included working at Ford Motor Company, being a Boy Scout executive, director of the Michigan Camping Association, owner and director of a summer camp and teacher. In Michigan, he taught science and math as well as serving as the director of the school planetarium. Upon their arrival in Orangeburg in 1978, Lois and Art hit the ground running. Their energy and zeal were unparalleled in all their civic involvements. They were avid volunteers with both boys and girls scouting programs. Mrs. Lusty's love of painting led to her hosting art classes at her home. Out of that came the formation of the Orangeburg League of Arts. She was very active with the I.P. Stanback Planetarium Advisory Committee, Girl Scouts, Newcomer's Club, Orangeburg Garden Club, Orangeburg Music Club and the Carolina Friendship Club.

Courtesy Orangeburg Fine Arts Center.

She also was responsible for the annual art exhibit in the statehouse lobby each year. She was named Orangeburg's Citizen of the Year in 1988.

Mr. Lusty served as chairman of the South Carolina State University Planetarium and the Orangeburg Beautification Committee. Because of his significant involvement with the Boy Scouts, he was the recipient of their highest honor, the Silver Beaver Award. In 1986, he was named Orangeburg's Citizen of the Year.

One of Art and Lois Lusty's greatest contributions was the establishment of the Orangeburg Arts Center. After noticing the old dilapidated river pavilion, they came up with the idea of turning it into a center to promote and display the arts of Orangeburg. After much work and hard labor, their dream became a reality in 1987.

Because of their many civic and volunteer endeavors, the governor named Art and Lois as the Volunteers of the Year in 1986 for South Carolina.

The Lustys were blessed with three children: Arthur J. Lusty III, Mary Lynne L. Chapman and Linda L. Becker. Mr. Lusty died in 1990, and Mrs. Lusty died in 2005. Orangeburg is forever indebted to the Lustys for their contributions and dedication toward the arts for our area.

H. Filmore Mabry (1928–1995)

Fil Mabry was an acknowledged leader in the field of hospital administration. His long tenure at the Regional Medical Center propelled our hospital into the forefront of healthcare.

Fil Mabry was born in Wilmington, North Carolina, in 1928 to Carl E. and Virginia B. Mabry. His education was obtained at the public schools in Greensboro. He graduated from Duke University in 1951, followed by a two-year tour of duty with the United States Marine Corps during the Korean War. Upon his return, he went back to Duke and obtained a master's degree in hospital administration in 1955.

His legendary career in hospital administration began as the administrator of the Clarendon County Memorial Hospital in Manning, South Carolina. In 1961, he came to be the leader at the Orangeburg Regional Hospital, a position he held until his 1993 retirement. While here, he made many significant improvements at the old Carolina Avenue facility, as well as oversaw the construction of a new state-of-the-art facility on St. Matthews Road. He propelled Orangeburg's hospital to the forefront of medicine, and his fiscal responsibility for the hospital was legendary.

Courtesy Joan Mabry.

Two of his greatest achievements were the construction of the new hospital and, later, the establishment of a cancer facility on the hospital campus. Appropriately, the hospital's board of trustees named this cancer facility in Mr. Mabry's honor for his outstanding leadership in healthcare.

Mr. Mabry was a longtime member of the South Carolina Hospital Association. He was also the recipient of its Distinguished Service Award in 1988. Because of his long and distinguished service, the association recognized him with an honorary life membership in 1994.

Civically, Mr. Mabry was a past president of the Rotary Club and a Paul Harris Fellow. As a young man, he achieved the rank of Eagle Scout. Religiously, he was very active at St. Andrew's United Methodist Church, being its administrative board chairman and chairman of the finance committee.

Fil Mabry married the former Joan Bryant, and they had four sons: Hank, Bryant, Don and Luke.

According to the South Carolina Hospital Association's president, Fil Mabry was "a true gentleman, a consummate statesman, and an acknowledged leader in the state's hospital field."

Reverend Dr. Hubert V. Manning (1918–1997)

For twenty-eight years, Dr. Hubert V. Manning guided the growth of Claflin University to new heights. His foresight to the needs of the future and his fundraising abilities were legendary.

Hubert Manning was born in Cheraw in 1918 to Reverend Irving V. and Fannie Manning. He spent most of his youth growing up in Pickens and Timmonsville. He graduated from Claflin College in 1940 and Gammon Theological Seminary in 1945. Dr. Manning received his master's degree from Boston University in 1948 and an honorary doctor of divinity degree from Gammon in 1957. He also did further study at the University of Michigan.

Ordained as a Methodist minister in 1940, he followed in his father's footsteps as a minister. He also was a member of the Claflin faculty from 1947 to 1951, where he taught history and religious education and was the college chaplain.

At the time of his selection as Claflin's president at age thirty-seven in 1956, he was serving as the pastor of Wesley Methodist Church in Charleston. He immediately began addressing two of the pressing needs of the school: reinvigorating and restructuring the faculty and rebuilding a dormitory that had been destroyed by fire. His "New Program" to do this, as well as improve Claflin's finances and physical plant, led Claflin to regain accreditation with the Southern Association of Colleges and Institutions. Dr. Manning's skills, energy and enthusiasm were a tremendous asset in revitalizing Claflin University.

Courtesy Claflin University.

During his tenure, the qualifications of faculty

members were greatly increased, the academic program was significantly improved, the physical plant was expanded tremendously with many new buildings and the student enrollment increased substantially. One of the highlights of his career came in 1967, when the newly constructed modern library was named the Hubert Vernon Manning Library for his tremendous leadership in guiding Claflin over the years.

In 1971, Boston University named him its Alumnus of the Year for his significant contributions to higher education. In 1976, Dr. Manning was named the president of the South Carolina Association of Colleges and Universities. After a long and significant career, he retired as the president of Claflin in 1984.

In 1946, Dr. Manning married the former Ethel Augusta Braynon, and they had two daughters: Dr. June Manning Thomas and Michelle Manning Henry. He died in 1997.

DR. HARRIS A. MARSHALL (1909–1968)

Harris A. Marshall devoted his entire professional career to public education in South Carolina. As the superintendent of the Orangeburg City Schools for thirteen years and the deputy superintendent for instruction at the State Department of Education, he cast a giant shadow in the field of education.

Harris Marshall was born in 1909 in Lydia, South Carolina, to Malvin and Ada Andrews Marshall. After attending the public schools there, he graduated from Furman University, where he was the student body president. Later, he received a master's degree in education from Duke University. Additionally, he did further study at Columbia University and the University of South Carolina.

Dr. Marshall taught at several schools as well as being a principal before becoming a superintendent of education at both the McColl and Darlington schools. In 1952, he became the superintendent of the Orangeburg City Schools, where he stayed until 1965, when he went to the State Department of Education to become the state's deputy superintendent of education. Because of his excellent management when in Orangeburg, in 1962 the board of trustees named the newest elementary school the Harris A. Marshall Elementary School.

During his career in education, Dr. Marshall served as president of the South Carolina High School League in 1943, the South Carolina Association of School Administrators in 1945 and the South Carolina Education

Association in 1955. He also served on the Southern Association of Colleges and Schools, which is the accrediting agency for schools in the South.

Courtesy Teresa Marshall.

Civically, he was president of the Kiwanis Club as well as the district lieutenant governor. He was active with the American Red Cross and was on the board of directors of the Crippled Children's Society and the Orangeburg Chamber of Commerce.

At First Baptist Church, he was a Sunday school teacher and served on the board of deacons.

Because of his outstanding professional reputation, an honorary doctor of laws degree was conferred upon him by his alma mater, Furman University, in 1963.

Dr. Marshall married the former Mary Hanna Hurst of Chesterfield, and they had two sons: Harris Jr. and Hurst. He died in 1968.

Dee H. McLafferty (1928–2001)

Dee McLafferty can be considered a pioneer in the field of head injury support groups. She not only founded the South Carolina Head Injury Association but also assisted in the creation of three other state organizations. Because of her leadership role, she has been honored nationally as well as being chosen as South Carolina's Mother of the Year in 1985.

Dee McLafferty was born and raised in Lincoln, Nebraska, in 1928. Her parents were Mr. and Mrs. Henry J. Hartmann. She graduated from the University of Nebraska with a degree in education and did graduate work at Western Kentucky University.

Courtesy Joel Hand.

In 1979, her son Kevin was seriously injured in an automobile accident that left him in a coma for six months as a result of traumatic brain injury (TBI). Over the next several years, she rarely left his side during his hospitalizations and rehabilitations in several cities across America. As a result, she became a state and national leader of the National Head Injury Foundation and began to help others with brain injuries, as well as their families. She led the efforts to establish statewide chapters in four states. Mrs. McLafferty prevailed upon South Carolina's governor to appoint a task force that later led to a comprehensive study of head and spinal cord injuries. This study led to the creation of the South Carolina Department of Disabilities and Special Needs in the early 1990s. Her testimony before federal agencies helped create a state registry for traumatic brain injury that became a nationwide model.

Earlier in her life, Mrs. McLafferty spearheaded the Selma, Alabama Charity League's major fundraiser, the Charity League Follies. During her life in Orangeburg, she was president of the Council of Garden Clubs, president of the Orangeburg Music Club and a board member of the Orangeburg Attention Homes, as well as being active in the Orton Dyslexia Society. She was highly regarded as a tutor of students with learning disabilities. Mrs. McLafferty was also very active in the Orangeburg Lutheran Church.

She married Charles (Chuck) McLafferty, and they had four children: Dr. Ardith McLafferty, Dr. Karen Foust, Dr. Charles McLafferty Jr. and Kevin McLafferty. She died in 2001.

Harold M. McLeod (1907–1999)

Harold McLeod has been a true civic servant. With over forty years of service with the Internal Revenue Service, he retired as the district director for all of South Carolina. Locally, he was a dynamo with his civic activities.

Harold McLeod was born in Timmonsville in 1907 to Dr. William R. McLeod and Ellen Boyd McLeod. He attended the public schools there and graduated from Wofford College in 1928. For the next four years, he was an elementary school teacher and administrator in Wellford near Spartanburg. Seeking a better-paying profession, he became a deputy collector for the IRS. Before long, he was chief of his division, overseeing more than forty deputies. In 1952, he became the assistant director of the IRS in South Carolina, and from 1960 until his retirement in 1973, he was the director for all of South Carolina.

He volunteered for service in World War II and served in various assignments, the last one being in Okinawa.

Courtesy Harold McLeod Jr.

Locally, Mr. McLeod was a member of the Salvation Army Advisory Board as well as the Orangeburg County Library Commission. As an avid volunteer with the United Way, he was the local and the state president as well as being named the 1975 South Carolina Volunteer of the Year. Mr. McLeod ably served the Lions Club as president in Anderson in his younger years and, later, as the president of the Orangeburg Lions Club. Active with the American

Legion, he was a past commander and was very involved with its Boys' State program and student oratory awards program. Ever the patriot, he was involved with the Sons of the American Revolution, where he served as a vice-president and general and national trustee. Mr. McLeod was the driving force behind the Orangeburg County Historical Society.

Mr. McLeod was very involved with his alma mater, Wofford College, where he served on the board of trustees from 1966 to 1978. For his outstanding service to Wofford, he was awarded a doctor of humanities degree in 1980. He and his wife also established the Harold M. and Carolyn B. McLeod Endowed Scholarship there in 1994.

Religiously, Mr. McLeod was very active at St. Paul's United Methodist Church, where he served in numerous leadership positions.

Mr. McLeod's financial skills were legendary. While a patient in intensive care at the local hospital at age ninety-one, his doctor found him propped up in bed diligently reading the *Wall Street Journal*. His explanation—he managed the retirement investments for several people and did not want to fall behind on any market changes.

Mr. McLeod married the former Carolyn Bowman, and they had two children: Harold M. McLeod Jr. and John B. McLeod. He died in 1999.

EARL M. MIDDLETON (1919–2007)

Earl M. Middleton was an Orangeburg icon. Not only was he a successful businessman, but he also ably served as the first Orangeburg African American member of the South Carolina House of Representatives since Reconstruction.

Earl Middleton was born in 1919 to Samuel E. and Ella Govan Middleton. He received his elementary, high school and college education at Claflin University. He served as his class president each year in college and graduated in 1942. During World War II, he served as a Tuskegee airman initially and later served in the Pacific Theatre. Upon his return from the war, he established a barbershop and gradually worked into selling insurance at his shop too. Later, due to his success in the insurance business, he phased out the barbering. Mr. Middleton added real estate services a few years later.

In 1974, Mr. Middleton was elected to South Carolina's House of Representatives, where he served for ten years.

In 1992, the *Wall Street Journal* recognized his entrepreneurial achievements with a front-page feature.

Courtesy Earl Middleton.

His ancestors grew up as slaves at Middleton Place Plantation in Charleston. Fittingly, Earl was asked in 1996 to be a trustee for the Middleton Place Foundation, where he served until his death. He was a founder of Boy Scout Troop 190 and helped lead this troop. For his many years in scouting, he received the prestigious Silver Beaver Award. Additionally, he led the efforts to found VFW Post 8166 in Orangeburg.

Among his many honors are the Order of the Palmetto, the Edisto Award from Orangeburg City Council, the Whitney Young Award from the Urban League, Orangeburg's Citizen of the Year in 2001, the 2003 HOPE Leadership Award in Real Estate and the Congressional Gold Medal from President Bush, which he received shortly before his death in 2007. His alma mater, Claflin University, gave him its T.K. Bythewood Award for his outstanding service.

Mr. Middleton faithfully served Claflin University as a member of its board of visitors and chairman of the first Capital Campaign in 1989. Claflin also bestowed him an honorary doctorate.

Mr. Middleton married the former Bernice Bryant, and they had three children: Anita M. Pearson, Kenneth E. Middleton and Karen M. Griffin.

Shortly before his death in 2007, he completed his autobiography. Also, the highway on which he lived was fittingly named the Earl M. Middleton Highway for his outstanding contributions to mankind.

ROY MIKELS (B. 1920)

As a founder and executive director of the Cooperative Church Ministries of Orangeburg (CCMO), Roy Mikels has been a godsend to help the poor in the Orangeburg area.

Born in 1920 in Pardee, Virginia, his family moved to western North Carolina when he was only seven months old. He received his elementary and high school education in Cullowhee, North Carolina. Afterward, his college career was at Mars Hill Junior College and at Western Carolina University, where he majored in business administration and accounting. After college, he entered the military in 1941 and served in Ireland, Scotland, North Africa and Italy. After World War II, he served as an accountant in Charlotte. In 1947, he came to Orangeburg to accept the position as accountant for Duncan Supply Company and the Duncan Hereford Farm, where he remained for nineteen years. In 1966, he became associated with Orangeburg's Department of Public Utilities as supervisor of the accounting department for ten years, followed by ten years as office manager.

Courtesy Roy Mikels.

It was during this time at DPU that he became aware of the multitude of problems facing a large population of the poor in the area. Upon his retirement, he joined a movement to combine the resources of area churches into one organization to help the poor. Thus, the CCMO was born. As one of the driving forces in its creation, he became the first executive director, a position he held for ten years. After that, he continued as board chairman for several more years as well as continuing to be a faithful volunteer. CCMO offers assistance to the poor with food, clothing, the purchase of medication, physician visits, rent payments and utility bills, as well as household items and furniture to those experiencing a fire loss. The entire operation is funded by area churches and donations, and all the staff is composed of volunteers. This program is probably the most significant of its type in this part of the state. Mr. Mikels has played a major role from its inception and is considered to be the driving force behind its success. Because of his endeavors with CCMO, Mr. Mikels was selected as Orangeburg's Citizen of the Year in 1993.

Civically, he was a longtime member of the Exchange Club and served two terms as president. Mr. Mikels has been a very active member at St. Andrew's United Methodist Church, where he has served as lay leader, administrative board chairman and a Sunday school teacher for forty-eight years. He was a certified lay speaker and was the district lay leader for the Orangeburg district.

In 1950, he married the former Dorothy Sandel, and they had three sons: Tommy, Bobby and Harold.

Mildred S. "Skip" Mutch (1916–1982)

As Orangeburg's legendary swimming instructor, Mrs. Mildred "Skip" Mutch taught over ten thousand people how to swim at the Edisto River swimming area.

Skip Mutch was born in 1916 to Charles and Mary Hummer Stelter. She grew up in Elizabeth, New Jersey, where her family had a wholesale produce business. During her youth, her family would shut down their business for a month each summer to go camping in national and state parks, where they fished, hunted, canoed, swam and enjoyed what the outdoors offered. As a teenager, she began to demonstrate her athletic prowess, excelling in swimming, diving, sprinting, basketball, field hockey and horseback riding.

After finishing Battin High School, she attended Centenary Collegiate Institute, a junior college in New Jersey. After graduating there, she went to Santa Barbara State College in California, where she graduated in 1939 in sociology and physical education. Later, she was certified at the National Aquatic School by some of the finest instructors in the country in swimming, diving, first aid, lifesaving, boating and canoeing.

Courtesy Carolyn Mutch.

After her marriage in 1940 to Harry Mutch, they lived in Detroit briefly while he was an engineer at Chrysler. When the United States entered World War II, they moved back to New Jersey, where he worked at a naval architectural firm. As she had worked for years as a camp counselor in water sports, her first permanent job was as the physical education instructor at the New Jersey State Penitentiary for Women. In 1947, Mr. Mutch became the sales manager in Orangeburg at the Southland Provision Co., also known as Azalea Meats. They started Mutch's Bakery here in 1948.

From 1949 to 1974, Skip Mutch taught swimming at the Edisto River swimming area as well as being director of water safety. With a firm but gentle hand, she taught hundreds of people, mostly youngsters, how to swim each summer. She would always arrive each day at the river in her traditional black bathing suit and high heels.

Mrs. Mutch's love for animals led her to be one of the mainstays of the Society for the Prevention of Cruelty to Animals in Orangeburg. Her efforts rescuing many abused, abandoned or injured animals was legendary. Horseback riding was another love in which she participated.

Skip Mutch and her husband, Harry, had three sons: Harry Jr., Carl and Ralph.

She always went full steam ahead with all that she did in life. Although she was only sixty-five when she died in 1982, many said that her life's odometer read one hundred years.

Dr. M. Maceo Nance Jr. (1926–2001)

Dr. Maceo Nance was the legendary president of South Carolina State College for almost twenty years. Facing many challenges, his leadership, wisdom and diplomatic skills propelled him into being the right man at the right time to lead South Carolina State College into the future.

Maceo Nance was born in 1926 to Milligan Maceo Nance Sr. and Louella Stewart Nance in Columbia. His high school education took place at Booker T. Washington. In 1942, he matriculated at South Carolina State College on a music scholarship, playing the trumpet. World War II interrupted his studies, and he served in the U.S. Navy from 1943 to 1946. Afterward, he returned and finished his education at SC State in 1949 with a degree in English. He furthered his studies at New York University, where he received a master's degree in 1953.

Dr. Nance's first employment was at the SC State ROTC supply room. Later assignments came at the bookstore and the Student Center. In 1959, he became the business manager at SC State, where he served until being named the vice-president for business and finance in 1967. Later in 1967, he was appointed as acting president. Faced with challenges in the aftermath of an unpopular president, he set about with a comprehensive plan to reinvigorate SC State. But this was interrupted in 1968 in the aftermath of a bowling alley protest that led to the death of three students. Dr. Nance's strong leadership was widely praised afterward, and he was named president in 1968, a position he held with distinction until his retirement in 1986. During that time, he turned the college around academically and physically. Facilities were upgraded, and many new buildings were

Courtesy Gene Atkinson.

built. One of his greatest assets was his "people skills" in leading SC State. Upon his retirement, he was bestowed with the title of president emeritus, a testament to his excellent leadership.

Maceo Nance married his college sweetheart, Julia Washington, and they had two sons: Maceo and Robert. He died in 2001 after many years of exceptional leadership and devotion to SC State. At his funeral, he was praised as a "man for all seasons" in leaving an indelible mark of progress at SC State.

R. PARK NEWTON JR. (1913–1988)

Industrialist, engineer, inventor, R. Park Newton Jr. was a leader in the nation and world with the company he founded, Applied Engineering Co. (APCO).

Mr. Newton was born in 1913 in Jackson, Georgia, to Robert Park and Bessie Powell Newton. After his early education there, he went to Georgia Tech, where he graduated with a degree in chemical engineering in 1935.

After various jobs in the engineering world, he came to Orangeburg in 1941 to be the executive vice-president at T.E. Wannamaker Chemical Co. During his tenure there from 1941 to 1945, the number of employees increased from 10 to 150.

Courtesy Lackey's Studio.

In 1945, Mr. Newton started out on his own by forming Applied Engineering Co. in Orangeburg. This industry began with Mr. Newton, a draftsman and a part-time secretary and served as an engineering consulting firm. After a year, the company branched out and began a sales representative operation, primarily for industrial boilers. It also designed and installed a number of turpentine-rosin plants as well as high-pressure ammonia systems for fertilizer plants.

In 1958, APCO entered the propane-air equipment field in designing, building and installing peak shaving plants for utility companies. By 1968, it was building more of these than all its competitors combined. Later, APCO spread into the international market with its engineering concepts and designs.

As time went on, its modular construction methods became very popular. Many patents were also obtained for its engineering concepts developed through the years. By the time Mr. Newton retired, Applied Engineering Co. had reached five hundred employees.

Park Newton was on the board of trustees for Orangeburg Regional Hospital, the board of directors of First National Bank, a director of the South Carolina Chamber of Commerce, a director and executive committee member of the United States Industrial Council, Who's Who in America and Who's Who in Commerce and Industry.

Mr. Newton married the former Elizabeth P. Edwards, and they had three children: Nancy, Park III and Aris. He died in 1988.

Rutledge L. Osborne (1895–1984)

State constitutional officer, University of South Carolina football coach, businessman, civic leader—Rut Osborne has done it all.

Rut Osborne was born in 1895 in Anderson to Rutledge L. and Louisa Gaillard Osborne. He received his early education there and his college education at Wofford College and the University of South Carolina. Athletic pursuits were dear to his heart, but Wofford had no athletic program, so the students organized their own teams there. During a baseball game, the Wofford group played the legendary Ty Cobb's touring team. Unfortunately, Ty Cobb and Mr. Osborne had a heated argument during the game that spilled over into a fight at a hotel room after the game.

When Wofford reestablished its football team, Rut Osborne was chosen as the captain. He transferred to the University of South Carolina for his senior year and played football while there. After college, he served with the National Guard on the Mexican border for six months. In 1918, Mr. Osborne, at age twenty-three, became the youngest person ever to serve as a South Carolina constitutional officer by being the state comptroller general. When the University of South Carolina's football coach left in the middle of the season in the early 1920s, Rut Osborne was asked to coach the team for the rest of the season, with no pay.

Courtesy Rut Osborne III.

From 1921 to 1939, Mr. Osborne worked with his brother-in-law in the W.A. Livingston Wholesale Co. grocery business. In 1946, he established the Orangeburg Realty Co.

Mr. Osborne is a former president of the Orangeburg Chamber of Commerce and the Rotary Club, former county chairman of the American Red Cross and was in charge of war bond drives during World War II. He served on the State Highway Commission and was chairman of the Orangeburg County Democratic Party as well as a delegate to the 1944 Democratic Party National Convention. He also established the first Boy Scout troop in Orangeburg.

Additionally, Mr. Osborne was a director of Southern National Bank and its successor, Bankers Trust. From 1947 to 1970 he served on the board of trustees for the University of South Carolina and was its chairman for eighteen of those years. Explosive growth in the physical plant and significant academic progress occurred during his tenure. For his exemplary service, USC conferred upon him the Algernon Sydney Sullivan Award, an honorary doctor of laws degree and its Distinguished Alumni Award in 1974, as well as electing him to its Athletic Hall of Fame. In 1973, the school's administrative building was named in his honor.

Mr. Osborne married the former Annie Lee Crum, and they had two sons: Rut Jr. and Bobby. He died in 1984 after a long career of distinguished service to our city and state.

Captain James C. Pace (1916–2009)

Captain J.C. Pace was an Orangeburg icon. His outgoing personality endeared him to many friends through the years.

J.C. Pace was born in 1916 in Sumter to Charles Wideman Pace and Frances Mallene Collins Pace. He grew up in Orangeburg and graduated from high school here. J.C. was very active in sports as a participant in early life, and he was a tremendous supporter of sports as an adult. He was a graduate of Bowling Green Business College. In the 1940s, he began his legendary thirty-nine-year career with the South Carolina Highway Patrol. When World War II came about, he served for three years in the United States Army. From 1972 to 1982, he served as the patrol commander for District 7. Known for his fairness, Captain Pace was highly respected by his colleagues.

Courtesy South Carolina Law Enforcement Officers' Hall of Fame.

A deeply religious person, Captain Pace served as the chaplain for the South Carolina Law Enforcement Officers Association and the chaplain emeritus of the South Carolina Troopers Association. He was also a deacon and elder at First Presbyterian Church in Orangeburg.

After his retirement from the patrol in 1982, he worked full time with Superior Motors in Orangeburg until age ninety.

Captain Pace was a Mason, a member of the Woodmen of the World and an Elk. He was a past president of the Kiwanis Club, served on the Salvation Army advisory board and the Albemarle Corporation Community Advisory Board and was a past commander of American Legion Post 4 and a past president of the South Carolina Law Enforcement Officers Association. Captain Pace was also very active with the Fellowship of Christian Athletes. In the 1980s, he was a recipient of the Order of the Palmetto for his outstanding service and also received the South Carolina American Legion Officer of the Year Award.

Two of Captain Pace's greatest loves were being an avid Clemson athletic fan and eating. Clemson's athletic booster club, IPTAY, bestowed the title of "Mr. Tiger" upon him. Regarding food, Captain Pace always had a knack for being a member of organizations where meals were served. When special cookouts occurred around town, he was a ready and willing participant.

Captain Pace married the former Audrey McCormick, and they had one daughter: Dree. He died in 2009 after a long career in law enforcement and civic accomplishments. He was a true friend to all he met.

Edward O. Pendarvis (1905–1992)

Edward O. "Eddie" Pendarvis was Orangeburg's longest-serving mayor, being in office from 1965 to 1989. As an honest and caring man, he was noted for his dignity, honor and integrity in guiding Orangeburg during those years.

Mr. Pendarvis was born in 1905 in the Fort Motte community to Timothy O. and Sallie Pendarvis. He was educated in the Calhoun County schools. After several early jobs, he opened the Paragon, a soda shop and drugstore, on the ground floor of the Eutaw Hotel in 1934. In 1940, he established the E.O. Pendarvis Candy and Tobacco Co., where he remained until his retirement in 1970.

Mr. Pendarvis was too young for service in World War I and too old for World II, so he served as an air raid warden in Orangeburg during World War II.

Prior to his election as mayor, he served for four years on city council, from 1961 to 1965. As mayor, he was always known for his consistent thoughtfulness for the best interest of all our citizens. He was a dedicated public servant and a capable leader. Mr. Pendarvis served during a time when industry was actively recruited to provide jobs for our economy. Additionally, the growth of the city-owned Department of Public Utilities increased tremendously

Courtesy City of Orangeburg.

during his tenure. After stepping down as mayor in 1989, City Council bestowed upon him the title of mayor emeritus.

Eddie Pendarvis was a member and past director of the Lions Club and a member of the Masonic order and the Elks. In 1989, the civic clubs of Orangeburg selected him as "Citizen of the Year" for his longtime service to the people of Orangeburg.

He was an active member at St. Paul's Methodist Church and served as treasurer of the Men's Bible Class there.

In 1933, Mr. Pendarvis married the former Clara Cook from Horry County, and they had three children: Shirley P. Guyton, Nancy P. Elliott and Edward O. Pendarvis Jr. He died in 1992.

Joyce W. Rheney (b. 1930)

As the South Carolina Mother of the Year in 2001 and a city councilwoman for twenty years, Joyce Rheney has devoted her life to civic service in Orangeburg.

Joyce Rheney was born in 1930 in Hartselle, Alabama, to William and Margaret L. White. She grew up in Athens, Alabama, and graduated from Athens High School. In 1949, she graduated from Jefferson-Hillman School of Nursing (now University of Alabama at Birmingham) in Birmingham, Alabama. As a RN, she was director of nurses at the tuberculosis sanitarium in Decatur, Alabama, as well as worked in the post-surgery unit at Roper Hospital and was pediatric head nurse at St. Francis Hospital in Charleston.

Courtesy City of Orangeburg.

After she and her husband moved to Orangeburg in 1954, she "retired" to a much more demanding life of raising four children.

Mrs. Rheney was very involved in many civic activities through the years. She has been an active member of the Medical Alliance, a volunteer in the nursery "Cuddle Care" at our local hospital and served on the Salvation Army board and the Low Country Planned Parenthood board. Mrs. Rheney was a past chairwoman of the Regional Medical Center's Foundation and has chaired its annual fundraising gala as well as chaired the Virginia Johnson Scholarship selection committee for nursing student scholarships.

Joyce Rheney was heavily involved with the restoration of Orangeburg's downtown venue, Stevenson Auditorium. She was co-chairwoman of coordinating all the decorating schemes during this renovation that was awarded the South Carolina Downtown Development Association's award for the best downtown renovation in South Carolina in 2001. Also in 2001, she was selected for the prestigious honor of South Carolina's Mother of the Year for her commitment to her family, her church and her civic deeds. In 1980, she was selected as the Clemson University Tiger Brotherhood Mother of the Year.

Mrs. Rheney served on the Orangeburg City Council from 1989 to 2009, where her commitment to Orangeburg produced many positive improvements.

She was a charter member of St. Andrew's United Methodist Church and has served on many committees there through the years.

Mrs. Rheney married Dr. John Rheney Jr., and they had four children: John III, Betsy, Bruce and David.

James W. Roquemore (b. 1955)

Jim Roquemore is quite a leader in the turf grass industry. As CEO of Patten Seed Co., he operates one of the largest diversified agricultural businesses in the South. The Super Sod division is one of the largest turf grass producers in the world.

Jim Roquemore was born in Lakeland, Georgia, in 1955 to William A. and Nell P. Roquemore. He attended Valdosta State College in Georgia.

Patten Seed Co. has been in existence since 1893, with Jim's great-grandfather as the founder. Jim became an integral part of the management team after college, and he has been guiding its reins since the death of his father in 1997. With about twenty thousand acres, Patten Seed Co. is one of America's largest sod and grass seed producers. The company also developed and owned eight Canongate Golf Clubs and country clubs with over eight thousand members altogether. Additionally, it has begun a tree nursery division in recent years.

Courtesy Jim Roquemore.

Jim Roquemore is a dynamo, not only in his profession but with his charitable, civic, community and organization activities as well. He is a director of the SCANA Corporation, a board member of South Carolina Bank and Trust and a member of the Southeast Region and National Boards of the Boy Scouts of America. Supporting scouting has been a major thrust in his life, as he has organized large fundraisers for this cause for many years. Mr. Roquemore has also been a member of the Coker College Board of Trustees, the Orangeburg Calhoun Technical College Board of Trustees, the President's Advisory Council at Clemson University, the Clemson Board of Visitors, past president of the Orangeburg County Chamber of Commerce, past president of the Rotary Club and board member of the Regional Medical Center Foundation.

Mr. Roquemore has received numerous awards for his endeavors through the years. Among these are the Order of the Palmetto, Orangeburg's Citizen of the Year in 1996, South Carolina's Ambassador for Economic Development in 2001 and the Boy Scouts Award of Merit, as well as the Silver Beaver Award.

Among Mr. Roquemore's hobbies and interests are hunting, fishing, flying, golf, softball and basketball.

He married the former Karen Bembry of Quitman, Georgia, and they are the parents of three children: Jay, Martha and Laura.

JUDGE LOUIS ROSEN (1910–1989)

A "judge's judge" is the way many have described Judge Louis Rosen. Fair, honest, gentlemanly and possessing a quick wit have been some of the descriptions of his life on the bench. His successor described him as "one of the best trial judges on the bench."

Louis Rosen was born in 1910 to Russian immigrants, Samuel and Bessie L. Rosen. He grew up in a one-room sharecropper's house near Awendaw in Charleston County. His father believed that education was the key to success in life and instilled this belief in all his children. Around age six, Louis and his family moved to Charleston so that he could attend a good school, but his Gullah and Yiddish dialect caused him to have to attend a school to teach him standard English first. Later in life, he quipped that he was the only person he knew who did not qualify for the first grade. As a boy growing up, he delivered newspapers barefooted as well as clerked in several Charleston stores to earn money.

Courtesy Debbie Rosen.

Louis Rosen later went to the University of South Carolina and graduated from the law school there with honors in 1934. Because of the hard times of the Depression, he and several classmates sometimes had to share a single chocolate bar as lunch. During school, he was hired as an errand boy for the Columbia city judge. Thus, the seeds were planted for his ultimate career.

In 1936, he came to work with the law firm of Lide and Felder in Orangeburg. As a hard worker, he arrived at work early and left late, even working weekends. World War II interrupted, and he served in the navy for four years. After the war, Mr. Rosen returned to Orangeburg and practiced law with Charlton Horger. In 1962 he was elected to serve as a judge in South Carolina's Circuit Court, perhaps one of the first to do so without prior service in the legislature. He ably served our court system for seventeen years.

Being a colorful judge, he also enjoyed the highest of reputations for his fairness and well-disciplined courtrooms.

Judge Rosen was a member of the Woodmen of the World, the Elks, the VFW, the American Legion and the Masonic lodge and a past president of the Rotary Club. He was well known as a resourceful raconteur and would captivate an audience wherever he might be.

Judge Rosen married the former Kathryn Limehouse, and they had two daughters and one son: Bonnie R. Moses, Dr. Deborah Rosen and Louis L. Rosen, who followed in his father's footsteps into the field of law. Judge Rosen died in 1989 after serving with distinction and honor during an outstanding career.

DR. GERALD E. RUNAGER (B. 1927)

Geb Runager has devoted his entire life to turning students and athletes into good citizens in Orangeburg. From coaching students in sports, to being an outstanding elementary school principal, to fostering the Fellowship of Christian Athletes program, Dr. Runager has been a dedicated and devoted person, building character and citizenship in the lives of young men and women.

Geb Runager was born in 1927 in Alabama to Fred B. and Ocie G. Runager. He grew up in Corbin, Kentucky, and received his secondary education there. He graduated from Erskine College in 1952, where he played on both the football and basketball teams. Dr. Runager furthered his education with a master's degree at the University of South Carolina and a doctorate degree at Nova University.

Courtesy Geb Runager.

After college, Geb Runager began his coaching career at Saluda High School. In 1958, he moved to Orangeburg to become the head basketball coach and two years later became the head football coach as well. In his first season as football coach, his Orangeburg High School team won the state championship. Then his basketball team went 21-0 in the regular season before losing in the state semifinals.

Dr. Runager left coaching in 1965 to work in sales for several years before returning to the Orangeburg schools as principal at Mellichamp Elementary and Marshall Elementary Schools, the latter for fifteen years until his unofficial retirement in 1993. Afterward, he was recalled twice to be an interim principal. In retirement, he still kept a hectic pace, being a volunteer kicking coach at South Carolina State University as well as helping area high school kickers. Additionally, he tutored his son Max in punting quite well, as he became a star punter at the University of South Carolina and for the San Francisco 49ers in the National Football League, even winning a coveted Super Bowl.

Coach Runager did not slow down his activities, even as he reached his eighties. For many years, he has been the middle school athletic director for the local public schools. He has also been the perennial chairman of the board for the local Fellowship of Christian Athletes.

Dr. Runager has been a teacher of the year, the North-South All Star head basketball coach, the South Carolina Football Coach of the Year in 1960, the Martin Luther King Community Service Award winner in 2006 and the Orangeburg Citizen of the Year in 2008.

At Orangeburg's First Presbyterian Church, he has served as a deacon, elder and choir member, as well as the moderator of the Charleston Atlantic Presbytery.

Dr. Runager married the former Nancy Culp, and they have five children: Mike, Pat, Max, Clark and Jane. Geb Runager has made an indelible impact on the lives of the youth of Orangeburg during his outstanding career.

Dr. Edward W. Rushton (1905–1998)

Dr. Ed Rushton cast a giant shadow upon Orangeburg. As a builder, he rebuilt the Orangeburg City Schools into an award-winning district. In addition, he literally built the Orangeburg County Council on Aging and its services from humble beginnings to become one of the top programs in the state.

Ed Rushton was born in 1905 in the little hamlet of Fork, South Carolina, to Reverend Jesse E. and Nora Lee Rushton. Most of his youth was spent in Branchville, where he attended the public schools. Dr. Rushton graduated from Wofford College in 1926 and later received a master's degree from the University of South Carolina and a doctorate degree from George Peabody College.

Courtesy Nancy Ayers.

After college, Dr. Rushton's first job was as a teacher and principal at Calhoun Falls. Next he went to Simpsonville to become its superintendent at age twenty-three. After seven years there, he went to be the superintendent at Batesburg-Leesville. In 1943, South Carolina's legislature voted to change the public schools from an eleven-year to a twelve-year system. Dr. Rushton was appointed state director for this new twelve-year program. This required revamping the entire education system, and he was sent to George Peabody College on a Rockefeller Foundation grant to study and devise a twelve-year curriculum plan for South Carolina.

From 1946 to 1952, Dr. Rushton was the superintendent of the Orangeburg City Schools. His rebuilding program garnered national attention and resulted in being awarded the best nationwide school system in the school and community improvement competition in 1951.

From 1952 to 1966, he was the superintendent of schools in Roanoke, Virginia. In 1966, he became the superintendent in Charlottesville, Virginia.

Dr. Rushton was also a consultant to the overseas schools of the United States State Department, as well as a lecturer at numerous colleges and universities. Upon his retirement in 1973, he moved back to Orangeburg, but actually he only changed gears, as he became a visiting professor at South Carolina State College. A few years later, he was appointed as the director of the Orangeburg County Council on Aging, a program that was just in its infancy. With his legendary administrative skills, he turned that organization around as well and expanded its services immensely. After eleven years there, and at age eighty-two, Dr. Rushton finally retired.

Dr. Rushton was a Rotarian and was honored as a Paul Harris Fellow. He was also selected for the hall of fame of the American Association of International Education. In 1981, he was honored as the Citizen of the Year in Orangeburg. At St. Paul's United Methodist Church, he served as a Sunday school teacher.

Ed Rushton married Lucille Roddey, and they had three children: Nancy R. Ayers, Eddie Rushton Jr. and Sally R. Miller. He died in 1998 after a distinguished career in education and improving the well-being of senior citizens.

Helen W. Sheffield (1898–1970)

Mrs. Helen Wilkinson Sheffield was an outstanding civic leader in Orangeburg. Her compassion for guiding the lives of children and adolescents was unparalleled.

Mrs. Sheffield was born in Orangeburg in 1898 to Dr. Robert S. Wilkinson, the second president of South Carolina State University, and Marion Birnie Wilkinson, who was quite a civic leader herself. Her early education was obtained at South Carolina State University, where she received a licentiate of instruction degree in 1919. In 1922, she received an AB degree from Atlanta University and a master's degree from New York University in 1936. Additional studies were done at Cornell University and Columbia University.

Mrs. Sheffield taught science and chemistry at South Carolina State University for thirty-nine years, from 1922 to 1961. She then became the full-time director of the Boarding Department. While at SC State, she was an advisor to many groups.

Mrs. Sheffield's civic accomplishments were numerous. She was a past president and executive secretary of the Sunlight Club, a federated women's club that ministered to children and youth; a member of the board of directors for both the United Fund and the Hospital Auxiliary; and vice-chairman of the Orangeburg Area Rehabilitation Center. She served on the Human Relations Council to promote cooperation and understanding between the races in Orangeburg. Mrs. Sheffield was key player in the formation of Orangeburg Community Action Agency and was also very active with the Girl Scouts program in Orangeburg. She also was a charter member of the Orangeburg chapter of Link's Inc., a benevolent civic organization. She served on the board of the Wilkinson Home for Girls, which was established by her mother in Cayce.

Although she was not blessed with children of her own, Mrs. Sheffield played the role of mother to many children throughout her life. She provided meaning and guidance in their lives. Because of her concern for the well-being of children, the Helen Sheffield Federated Girls' Club was named in her honor.

Mrs. Sheffield was married to Frederick Sheffield. Unfortunately, she died in 1970 in an automobile accident while doing what she loved best, as she was transporting children home from an afternoon session at the Sunlight Club. She was indeed a ray of sunlight in the lives of many children in Orangeburg.

DR. HILLA SHERIFF (1903–1988)

Dr. Hilla Sheriff has been referred to as "the Grand Dame of South Carolina Public Health." Her zeal and dedication led her to do more to improve public health in South Carolina than any other person.

Hilla Sheriff was born in 1903 near Easley, South Carolina, to John W. and May Lenora Sheriff. Her family moved to Orangeburg, where she spent her childhood years. After graduating from Orangeburg High School in 1920, she went to the College of Charleston. After two years there, she matriculated at the Medical College of South Carolina, where she graduated in 1926. Dr. Sheriff interned in Philadelphia and then did a residency for two years at Children's Hospital in Washington, D.C., and the Willard Parker Contagious Disease Hospital in New York City.

In 1929, she established a pediatric practice in Spartanburg and conducted volunteer clinics at the Spartanburg County Health Department. In doing so, she became hooked on public health medicine and became the department's director. Dr. Sheriff established significant programs to reduce the death rate from pellagra and tuberculosis as well as to control venereal disease through

Courtesy South Caroliniana Library.

education. Immunization programs, prenatal and postnatal clinics and school hygiene programs also were established.

In 1936, Dr. Sheriff received a Rockefeller Foundation fellowship to study public health at Harvard University, where she received a master's degree in 1937. In 1941, she became the director of maternal and child health for the South Carolina Health Department. By the time she retired in 1974, she was deputy commissioner of the South Carolina Department of Health and Environmental Control.

Dr. Sheriff received many honors and awards throughout her career: the first recipient of the Ross Award for outstanding service in maternal and child health from the Southern Branch of the American Public Health Association, the Meritorious Award of the South Carolina Mental Health Association, South Carolina's Outstanding Female Employee of the Year in 1974, the Order of the Palmetto, the Distinguished Alumna Award from the Medical University of South Carolina and the prestigious William Weston Distinguished Service Award for Excellence in Pediatrics in South Carolina.

Dr. Sheriff married Dr. George H. Zerbst, who also was deeply involved with public health. She died in 1988 after an illustrious career in public health, where she established some of the most important standards for the state of South Carolina.

Hugo S. Sims Jr. (1921–2004)

Hugo Sims Jr. was an Orangeburg icon in the business and banking world. As a soldier in World War II, he was hailed as an outstanding hero.

Courtesy Ginger Risher.

Hugo Sims Jr. was born in Orangeburg in 1921 to Hugo S. and Lucile H. Sims. His father was a giant in the legal, journalistic and educational world. His mother was South Carolina's Mother of the Year in 1959. Hugo was educated in the Orangeburg City Schools and graduated from Wofford College in 1941 and the University of South Carolina Law School in 1947.

As a paratrooper who parachuted behind the German lines in France on D-Day, he was recognized as a war hero. For his actions leading the "Incredible Patrol," he received the Distinguished Service Cross, the Silver Star and the Bronze Star, as well as citations from France, Belgium and the Netherlands.

In 1946, as a law student, Mr. Sims was elected to the South Carolina House of Representatives for a two-year term. In 1948, at age twenty-eight, he was elected to the United States House of Representatives, where he served for two years.

In Orangeburg, he practiced law, was the city attorney and founded Management and Investment Co., a real estate investment firm. He was a founder and chairman of the Orangeburg National Bank and its parent company, Community Bankshares. This venture also led to the development of Sumter National Bank and Florence National Bank.

Mr. Sims was very involved in education and served on the Orangeburg School District 5 board of trustees, as well as the boards of Claflin and Wofford Colleges. Wofford conferred an honorary doctor of laws degree upon him in 1991. Civically, he was very involved with the Rotary Club, the American Red Cross, the Boy Scouts and the United Way. He was selected as Orangeburg's Citizen of the Year in 1954 by all the civic clubs.

Mr. Sims was a charter member of St. Andrew's Methodist Church. He married Virginia Bozard, and they had three children: Hugo Sims III, Ginger S. Risher and Cal Sims. Hugo Sims died in 2004 after an incredible career serving the business and financial world in Orangeburg.

Lucile H. Sims (1894–1994)

In being selected as South Carolina's Mother of the Year in 1959, Mrs. Lucile Sims has certainly been a role model for civic activity in Orangeburg.

Mrs. Sims was born in 1894 in Orangeburg to Charles L. and Jessie Smoak Howell. She received her education at Orangeburg's public schools and Winthrop College. She taught school for several years afterward.

After her marriage in 1917, Mrs. Sims began to write feature columns for her husband's Editor's Copy, a nationwide newspaper syndicate that eventually included over five hundred newspapers. Additionally, she was the society editor of the weekly newspaper, the *Orangeburg Sun.*

During the Depression in the 1930s, Mrs. Sims opened a private kindergarten and taught children there for seven years. Because of her devotion to the unfortunate, she was instrumental in the establishment and operation of the Orangeburg Day Nursery for underprivileged children for many years. Mrs. Sims also helped create improved conditions for South Carolina's juvenile jails as well as a separate juvenile court system with its own probation officers.

Courtesy Orangeburg County Historical Society.

During World War II, Lucile Sims was chairman of the Women's Civil Defense unit in Orangeburg. She also served as a director of the Red Cross and a volunteer with the Orangeburg Regional Hospital's "Gray Ladies." She was chairman for the Tuberculosis Association's annual fundraising drive and was a past president of the Orangeburg chapter of the Winthrop Daughters. She was a devoted member of St. Paul's Methodist Church, where she taught Sunday school for nearly fifty years.

With an interest in the theatre, Mrs. Sims was a leader and past president of the Town Players in Orangeburg. As an active participant in the Orangeburg Garden Club, she was a past state treasurer and state historian for the Garden Clubs of South Carolina. In 1959, she was selected as South Carolina's Mother of the Year.

Lucile Sims was married to Hugo S. Sims Sr., and they had three sons: Hugo Jr., Edward and Henry II. Mrs. Sims was a champion for all people and will always be remembered for her many efforts to make Orangeburg a better place. She died at age one hundred in 1994.

W. EUGENE SMITH (1915–1982)

W. Eugene Smith was a renowned educator in Orangeburg. His colleagues have referred to him as a "principal's principal," as his ideas were years ahead of everyone else in the educational world.

Gene Smith was born in Punxsutawney, Pennsylvania, in 1915 to Chauncey C. and Veda R. Smith. He attended college in Pennsylvania at Grove City College and graduated from Erskine College in Due West, South Carolina, in 1939. While in college, he was president of the Literary Society and played football, basketball and ran track. Mr. Smith did further graduate education at North Carolina State University, Appalachian State Teachers College and the University of South Carolina.

After college, his first employment was at Hendersonville High School in North Carolina from 1939 to 1943, where he was a teacher, coach and vocational education guidance counselor. During World War II, he was a physical education instructor for the Army Air Corps at Lynchburg College, Virginia, as well as served in the navy.

Mr. Smith was the principal at Cope High School in 1946–47. He then came to Orangeburg High School as a teacher, coach and director of student activities. He assumed the duties of principal in 1953 and was considered to be an outstanding administrator who was years ahead of his time. He led the South Carolina Association of Secondary Principals as its secretary treasurer and president. Mr. Smith was a founder and executive secretary of

Courtesy Bob Smith.

the South Carolina Association of Student Councils. He was considered to be a pioneer in developing students' citizenship skills with their involvement in student councils. His talents placed him on numerous committees with the South Carolina Education Association over the years. Mr. Smith was also on the National Council for National Honor Societies.

Mr. Smith left Orangeburg High School in 1964 to become the supervisor of history and social studies for the South Carolina State Department of Education. Subsequently, he became the supervisor for secondary education for South Carolina until his retirement in 1981.

Gene Smith was a past president of the Lions Club, a past president of the Orangeburg County Education Association and a leader of many charitable community fundraising drives, as well as a member of the Red Cross Executive Board.

At the Episcopal Church of the Redeemer in Orangeburg, he served as the secretary of the vestry.

Mr. Smith married the former Bivens Ashe, and they had two children: Robert L.A. Smith and Bivens S. Rinehart. He died in 1982 after a superlative career in education.

FRANK M. STALEY JR. (B. 1929)

As a jovial referee and umpire for many years, Frank Staley always kept athletic games under control with his humor and wise officiating. As a leader in scouting, he was a mentor to many young men, teaching them about character and values in life.

Frank M. Staley Jr. was born in 1929 to Frank M. Staley Sr. and Sarah Ryan Staley. Before his 1946 graduation from A.S. Staley High School in Georgia, he readily participated in the school's football, basketball and baseball programs. In 1951, he received a BS degree in mathematics from South Carolina State College and then a master's degree from Columbia University in 1955. Mr. Staley received further math education at several other colleges and universities through the years.

Mr. Staley served on active duty in the United States Army from 1951 to 1954 as well as participating in the Army Reserves for many years. During that time, he furthered his military education at numerous service schools. Among these were Air War College, Field Artillery School, Ordnance School, Intelligence School and the National War College.

In the civilian world, he taught mathematics at Fort Valley State College in Georgia and Virginia State College in Petersburg, Virginia, before coming to South Carolina State in 1958. He was an integral part of the mathematics department there until his retirement in 1990. One of Mr. Staley's best loves was sports, which helped launch his career as a legendary referee and umpire. As an official, he served from the recreational level all the way up to the college level. He always made the games he officiated entertaining with his humorous gesticulations while making accurate calls. At his pinnacle, he was a

Courtesy Gene Atkinson.

renowned official in the Atlantic Coast Conference, the Eastern Athletic Association and several other conferences.

Locally, he has mentored many Boy Scouts as a scoutmaster and regional scout leader. He has been honored with the Silver Beaver Award and the Award of Merit. Civically, Mr. Staley has been a past chairman of the Orangeburg County Department of Social Services and the Red Cross board of directors. He is a member of the VFW and the American Legion.

Mr. Staley has been selected to several halls of fame, including the Naismith Memorial Basketball Hall of Fame, the South Carolina Officials' Basketball Hall of Fame, the South Carolina State University Athletic Hall of Fame and the ROTC Hall of Fame.

He married the former Valeria Howard, and they had two children: Frank and Elisa.

James E. Sulton (1923–2008)

Jim Sulton was a pioneer in the civil rights movement in Orangeburg in the 1950s and 1960s. Although at the forefront, he never sought recognition or accolades for his leadership. As time went on, he spent much energy on many community-minded projects to make Orangeburg a better place in which to live.

Courtesy Gene Atkinson.

Jim Sulton was born in Orangeburg in 1923 to McDuffie and Bessie Sulton. He completed the high school program at Claflin University and went to Morehouse College in Atlanta, Georgia. When World War II intervened, he served in the United States Army. While in service, he experienced a pivotal moment when a German prisoner of war told him how he was a fool to fight for a country in which he had no rights. From that moment on, he committed himself to help with the civil rights movement and its endeavors.

While growing up, he helped his father and uncle in their J.J. Sulton and Sons lumber business. From these experiences, he learned that hard work and perseverance were the core values of being successful in life. When he returned from World War II, the economic conditions were not favorable for him to join the family business. Therefore, he and his brother Roy opened up an Esso service station at the corner of Russell and Buckley Streets. It was the first minority-owned service station in Orangeburg, and they operated it for nearly thirty years. After that, they diversified into the fuel oil business.

During the civil rights era, Jim Sulton led protest marches, coordinated voter registration drives and participated in sit-ins at lunch counters. He also housed the Reverend Dr. Martin Luther King Jr. when he came to Orangeburg to give a speech.

Later in life, he became a founding member of the Edisto Habitat for Humanity and helped establish the headquarters and adjacent workshop for the Association of Retarded Citizens, now known as the Special Needs Board. Mr. Sulton was co-chairman of the Orangeburg Cemetery Committee to restore the historic African American cemetery in town, and he served as the co-chairman of Project Hope, an organization dedicated to racial harmony and understanding in Orangeburg. In 2006, he was named the Citizen of the Year in Orangeburg for his many years of making a pronounced difference to help improve Orangeburg.

Jim Sulton married the former Ruby Clowers, and they had five children: Cindy, James Jr., Francis, Christopher and Thomas. He died in 2008. Mr. Sulton will always be remembered as an unsung hero whose actions and deeds made life better for all.

Anabel H. Summers (1904–2005)

Mrs. Anabel H. Summers was a community coordinator for many causes throughout her life. From her leadership with the Red Cross to the Mental Health Association, she was the consummate community leader in these and other benevolent causes.

Mrs. Summers was born in Cross Hill in Laurens County in 1904 to Archie M. and Jesse R. Hill. Her early education was obtained there, and she was the valedictorian of her high school class. She graduated from Coker College in Hartsville in 1924, where she was the student body president and May Queen.

Courtesy Tom Summers.

Anabel Summers's working career began in Orangeburg in 1925 at the local Highway Department. She boarded in a home that was next door to her future husband.

In the late 1930s, she was president of the Ellis Avenue PTA and served on the state PTA executive committee. During World War II, she was the county chairman for all Red Cross volunteers. This duty included organizing and coordinating the first aid programs, the canteen services, handbags for hospitals, the motor corps and nurses' aide groups. Additionally, she served as the chair of the Women's Division of the Orangeburg County Council of Defense. From 1944 to 1946, Mrs. Summers was the executive secretary of the Orangeburg County Red Cross Chapter. In 1951, she was selected as one of twenty women to serve on a national planning committee in Washington, D.C. for the American Red Cross. She also served as the executive secretary of the Orangeburg County Tuberculosis Association from 1953 to 1959. As a lifelong volunteer with the Orangeburg County Mental Health Association, she participated in a two-mile Mental Illness Awareness Walk at age eighty-nine in Columbia.

Mrs. Summers was a leader in her church women's circle group at St. Paul's Methodist Church for many years. Interestingly, she walked a mile a day until age ninety-six.

She married Carroll Summers, an Orangeburg lawyer and later the Orangeburg County judge, and they had two sons: Carroll Summers Jr. and Reverend Tom Summers. She died in 2005 at age 101. Mrs. Summers was known for her everlasting thoughtfulness to those in need.

JUDGE CARROLL E. SUMMERS (1901–1992)

Judge Carroll Summers spent his lifetime in Orangeburg dispensing the law as well as participating in many civic deeds.

Carroll Summers was born in Orangeburg in 1901 to Abram West and Caroline Moss Summers. He graduated from Orangeburg High School and then Trinity College (now Duke University) in 1923. Afterward, he attended the law school at the University of South Carolina for two years, read law at the firm of Lide and Felder and was admitted to the bar in 1926. Mr. Summers practiced law in Orangeburg from 1926 to 1951 and became the Orangeburg County judge in 1951, where he served until 1973.

Courtesy Tom Summers.

Mr. Summers developed the Moss Heights residential area along with his brother West Summers in the 1920s and 1930s. It was Orangeburg's first planned subdivision. He was instrumental in encouraging the city to hire a professional horticulturalist to rejuvenate Edisto Gardens in 1937. He also helped organize the Memorial Park Cemetery on Broughton Street in the 1930s.

For many years, Judge Summers served on the Orangeburg County Board of Education, as well as for twenty years on the City Recreation Commission. During World War II, he was a member of the Home Guard and also chaired the Orangeburg County Rationing Board. Judge Summers was on the board of directors of Orangeburg Building and Loan Association and served as its vice-president. Religiously, he was a longtime teacher of the Men's Bible Class at St. Paul's Methodist Church. Additionally, he served as chairman of the board of trustees for the entire South Carolina Methodist Conference in the 1950s.

Judge Summers was well known for his gardening talents. He maintained a vegetable and fruit garden as well as grew roses and camellias to beautify his yard.

He married the former Anabel Hill from Cross Hill, South Carolina, and they had two sons: Carroll Summers Jr. and Reverend Tom Summers. He died in 1992 at age ninety-one.

Thomas S. Summers (1903–1974)

As a creative innovator, Tom Summers founded the first pilots' breakfast club in America in Orangeburg, which led to a nationwide trend. Additionally, he helped found the Sportsman's Club, which gave boat rides on the Edisto River as a fundraiser for the Crippled Children's Society of South Carolina.

Tom Summers was born in Cameron in 1903 to Dr. Samuel J. and Hester K. Summers. He received his education in the public schools in Cameron.

Mr. Summers operated a notable jewelry store in Orangeburg for almost fifty years. The flying bug bit him in the early days of aviation, and he was one of the first people to own an airplane at the Orangeburg airport in the 1930s. He conceived the idea to start a pilots' breakfast club in 1938, in which South Carolina airplane owners would fly to a designated city every other Sunday to meet, share fellowship and, of course, eat breakfast together. This was the first of its kind in the United States, and the word spread quickly across the nation, which led to pilots' breakfast clubs being formed in every state.

Mr. Summers was also one of the driving forces behind the formation of the Sportsman's Club in 1950. This was a group of Orangeburg boating enthusiasts who came together at first to share their boating hobby as well

Courtesy Sylvia Boone.

as to help clean up the Edisto River for boating in the area around Edisto Gardens. This led to the club offering boat rides during the Sundays around Easter to raise funds for the Crippled Children's Society of South Carolina. They did this for many years during the 1950s and 1960s.

Mr. Summers also organized a bowling club and a boxing club in Orangeburg. He was a member of the Kiwanis Club as well as being a Shriner.

For his contributions to aviation, he was posthumously inducted into the South Carolina Aviation Hall of Fame in 2000.

Mr. Summers married the former Kitty Way, and they had two children: Sylvia S. Boone and Reverend Tom Summers Jr. He died in an automobile accident in 1974. His contributions to the flying and boating enthusiasts' organizations were immeasurable.

DR. HENRY N. TISDALE (B. 1944)

Dr. Henry N. Tisdale has been the visionary president of Claflin University from 1994 to the present. His energetic leadership and guidance have led Claflin through a tremendous surge in growth not only in academics but with the physical plant too.

Henry Tisdale was born in Kingstree in 1944 to Walter and Willar M. Tisdale. He attended the public schools in Kingstree and was the valedictorian of his graduating class at St. Mark School in 1961. At Claflin University,

Courtesy Claflin University.

he graduated magna cum laude in the class of 1965. He received a master's degree in education at Temple University and a master's degree as well as a doctor of philosophy degree in mathematics at Dartmouth College.

Dr. Tisdale served in several capacities at Delaware State University during his twenty-four-year tenure there. Among these were assistant dean for administration, senior vice-president and chief academic officer.

In 1994, Dr. Tisdale was selected to become president of his alma mater, Claflin University. He hit the ground running and propelled Claflin to significant heights. Enrollment increased nearly 70 percent, and new academic programs at both the undergraduate and graduate levels were established. The physical plant has been transformed tremendously, with many new buildings as well as renovation and upgrading of existing facilities. Picturesque landscaping and award-winning new entrances, along with construction of the beautiful Legacy Plaza, have greatly enhanced the presentation of the campus.

In 2008, Forbes.com listed Claflin as the top historically black college or university in the United States as well as ranked Claflin in the top 4 percent in the rankings of "America's Best Colleges." *U.S. News and World Report* has ranked Claflin in the "Top Ten" among institutions in the South for over ten years.

Dr. Tisdale has received numerous awards and honors. Among these are the I. DeQuincy Newman Humanitarian Award, the 2007 Milliken Medal of Quality Award, the NAACP Educator of the Year Award, the Dartmouth Fellow Award and the DuPont Faculty Award.

Henry Tisdale married the former Alice Carson, and they have two children: Danica C. Tisdale and Brandon K. Tisdale.

FRANK P. TOURVILLE SR. (B. 1933)

As an industrialist, Frank Tourville has had a profound impact on Orangeburg. As a philanthropist, he has touched many facets of life in Orangeburg. His significant reinvigoration of the Orangeburg Country Club has had an unprecedented effect on the recruitment of industry and the social welfare of the people of Orangeburg.

Frank P. Tourville was born in 1933 in Burlington, Vermont, to Charles and Irene Tourville. He grew up in South Hero, Vermont, and graduated from Milton High School in Milton, Vermont. He served in the United States Army from 1953 to 1956 in the Combat Engineers Division. Later, he furthered his education at Morris County College in New Jersey.

Mr. Tourville began his career in the fluoropolymer industry in 1956 at American Supertemp Wire in Winooski, Vermont. Starting as an extrusion operator, he was quickly promoted into management because of his abilities. Later, he accepted positions with two other companies before starting out on his own. By then, he had seen how poor customer service and inadequate business decisions could affect the success of a company.

Courtesy Zeus, Inc.

In 1966, he established Zeus Industrial Products in Raritan, New Jersey. At that time, the entire production force consisted of Mr. Tourville and one employee in an old warehouse with minimal lighting and no heat or air conditioning. Zeus's dedication to producing a quality product led to its steady growth over the years.

In 1981, Zeus expanded to Orangeburg, and the rest is history. It has grown into one of the world's leaders in extruding high-performance fluoroploymer tubing such as Teflon. Zeus's products are used in multiple applications in the aerospace, medical device, semiconductor, automotive and petroleum markets. Products are customized for each customer's specific needs. Growth has been so phenomenal that Zeus has manufacturing locations in Raritan, New Jersey; Orangeburg, Aiken and Gaston, South Carolina; and Ireland. It has more than one thousand employees, and sales representatives are located throughout the world.

Mr. Tourville has received many honors and awards. Among these are the Links, Inc. Humanitarian Award in 2001, the DuPont "Whitey" Bro Lifetime Achievement Award in 2002, the Edisto Award in 2002 from Orangeburg City Council, the Orangeburg Touchdown Club Community Service Award in 2006, the South Carolina Ambassador of Economic Development Award in 2006 and the Martin Luther King Service Award in 2008.

When the Orangeburg Country Club was facing being closed in 2009, Mr. Tourville took over the ownership and assumed its indebtedness. He made gargantuan improvements to the golf course and significantly upgraded the rest of the facilities to make it one of the finest clubs in the Southeast.

Frank Tourville and his wife, Pearl, are the parents of four sons: Frank Jr., Jeff, Mike and Doug. Mr. Tourville is to be commended for his industrial impact and for his attentiveness and philanthropy for the well-being of Orangeburg.

Bernice W. Tribble (b.1938)

As the energetic leader behind the Downtown Orangeburg Revitalization Association (DORA), Bernice Tribble has been a dynamo behind the revitalization of Orangeburg's downtown business area.

Mrs. Tribble was born in Easley, South Carolina, to William Harrison Williams and Annie Lou H. Williams. She received her education in the Easley public schools and at Mars Hill College.

Bernice Tribble served as the executive director of the Marlboro County Arts Council and chairman of the Clio, South Carolina Beautification Committee. At the latter, she received a nationwide award for Outstanding City Development at the Kennedy Center in Washington, D.C., for organizing a revitalization effort with one hundred volunteers painting the downtown storefronts.

Upon her move to Orangeburg, she became the executive director of the Orangeburg County Arts Center. In 1996, she became the executive director for DORA. Under her leadership, DORA has received twenty-six statewide

Courtesy Bernice Tribble.

awards. She has led the effort to rejuvenate downtown with façade grants for businesses, organized fundraising events to create more downtown parking lots, created the Taste of Orangeburg and spearheaded the exceptional streetscape renovations. Her contagious enthusiasm has helped propel downtown from a deteriorating state to a new level of vibrancy.

Mrs. Tribble is a past president of the Morning Rotary Club as well as a founding member of the Community of Character program. She and her husband helped organize the Relay for Life as a fundraiser for the American Cancer Society. She has been a member of the executive committee for the Regional Medical Center Foundation, a board member of the Fellowship of Christian Athletes and a trustee of the Dick Horne Foundation.

Bernice Tribble received the Martin Luther King Community Service Award in 2005, the Order of the Silver Crescent (South Carolina's highest award for community service) in 2005 and the Boys and Girls Club Thomas Eklund Community Service Award in 2009. In 2002, she was chosen as Orangeburg's Citizen of the Year.

Bernice Tribble is married to Don Tribble, and they have three children: Brian Tribble, Tracy T. Caulder and Todd Tribble.

Lillie Mae Tyler (1924–1993)

Orangeburg has been blessed, and the nursing profession has been blessed, with the spirit of Florence Nightingale as revealed through Mrs. Lillie Mae Tyler. Her compassion and caring for the sick were unparalleled.

Lillie Mae Tyler was born in Kinder, Louisiana, in 1924 to John F. Anderson and Della C. Anderson. Always feeling compelled to care for the sick, she went to Appalachian Hospital School of Nursing in Johnson City, Tennessee, where she graduated in 1947. She earned her bachelor's degree in social studies and teaching certificate from East Tennessee University in 1954, as well as a master's in education there in 1957.

Mrs. Tyler came to Orangeburg in 1962 to become the director of the nursing school at Orangeburg Regional Hospital, a position she held for

Courtesy Regional Medical Center.

seventeen years. During her tenure, she was commended for carrying the nursing program to greater heights. For several years, she volunteered her time during holidays to help in the rural impoverished coal mining towns in Appalachia by working through the Red Bird Mission in its hospitals.

In 1979, she was led to do mission work with the Methodist Church full time and was sent to Espanola, New Mexico, to serve as a staff nurse in the hospital in that indigent area. In 1990, she returned to Orangeburg to establish its first hospice program. Her energy and drive guided this much-needed program in its infant years. She worked diligently, procuring private support to make this program become a viable entity.

Through the years, Mrs. Tyler has received numerous awards and honors. Among these are the Most Outstanding Volunteer of the Year Award in the Bell County, Kentucky school system, the Outstanding Older American Award and the J.C. Penney award for the Spirit of the American Woman. In 1992, she was chosen as Orangeburg's Citizen of the Year for her many years of dedication and compassion for the healthcare needs of the sick.

Lillie Mae Tyler was married to Lewis H. Tyler, who unfortunately died of cancer early in their marriage. Mrs. Tyler also died of cancer at the age of sixty-nine in 1993. In true fashion, her compassion for others was exhibited just a few days before her death, when she stayed up half the night caring for an elderly lady at the Methodist Home who had experienced surgery earlier in the day.

C. Frederic Ulmer (1913–1980)

C. Frederic Ulmer was the legendary chorus director at Orangeburg High School for many years. The annual operettas he showcased at the old Carolina Theatre were the cultural highlights each year in Orangeburg.

Fred Ulmer was born in Cameron in 1913 to Thomas Frederic and Minnie Richardson Ulmer. His elementary and high school education was obtained there. After high school, he worked at a combination service station and grocery store for four years. During this time, his interest in music began to appear, as he learned how to play the piano. His mother always wanted him to procure a college education, so he entered Furman University; however, he returned home after his first year due to the death of his father. But his mother was insistent that he complete his degree, so he returned on a scholarship and graduated with a degree in English and a minor in music.

Afterward, Mr. Ulmer was employed in Union, South Carolina, where he taught English and history. During the afterschool hours, he helped organize

Courtesy Warrior yearbook.

and direct the first boys' glee club in the school's history.

In 1940, he began his legendary career at Orangeburg High School, where he remained for thirty-two years teaching vocal music. The Mixed Chorus that he directed achieved stellar heights in the music world with its stage productions and musicals. Beginning in 1948, the annual operettas played to sold-out performances every year. During the 1950s, the Mixed Chorus, under his direction, sang on live television every year in Columbia on Christmas morning.

Mr. Ulmer furthered his education at Westminster College in Princeton, New Jersey, the University of South Carolina and received a master's degree in music from Columbia University in New York.

He was a devout member of Cameron Baptist Church, where he served as a deacon, organist and choir director.

Tragically, Mr. Ulmer and his twin sister died from injuries received in an automobile accident in 1980. The piano accompanist for many of his musical productions, Mrs. Betty Jo Fersner, summed up Mr. Ulmer best in a letter to the local newspaper afterward:

> *Frederic Ulmer gave the community of Orangeburg some of its finest moments. He didn't just reach our children—he encouraged them to reach for the stars. He gave of himself totally, dedicating himself to his students and instilling in them a love of music, high moral standards, a pride in themselves, and a respect for their fellow man. There are many adults in our town who are outstanding citizens because this giant of a man touched and enriched their lives.*

JAMES F. WALSH (1915–2003)

As a banker and outstanding civic servant, James F. Walsh was an Orangeburg icon. He dedicated his entire life to leadership of community, eleemosynary and civic endeavors.

James F. Walsh was born in Orangeburg County to Emmet and Mamie L. Walsh. His early education was obtained in the North public schools, and he graduated from the University of South Carolina in 1937. After working on his father's farm for a short while, he was asked by Southern National Bank to fill in for an employee who had surgery. Except for two years when he had to take over the family farm upon his father's death, he stayed at the bank until his retirement forty-two years later. At that time, he was the Orangeburg city executive for the bank's successor, Bankers Trust.

Mr. Walsh was heavily involved with his community endeavors. He was a past president of the Chamber of Commerce, the local Red Cross chapter, the American Cancer Society, the United Way and the Kiwanis Club. Additionally, he was the Kiwanis district lieutenant governor. He served for twelve years as chairman of the North School District's board of trustees. In 1962, he was the state president of the South Carolina Association of School Boards. Mr. Walsh also served on the board of trustees of the Regional Medical Center, the local hospital.

Courtesy James F. Walsh Jr.

Mr. Walsh was an organizer of the Limestone Rural Water District and served on the board of the Lower Savannah Council of Governments.

In 1954, he became the first treasurer of the Methodist Home for the Aging, a position he held for nearly forty years. Because of his commitment there, the large apartment building constructed in 1994 was named the James F. Walsh Building.

Mr. Walsh ably served Orangeburg County as a county councilman from 1980 to 1988. In 1984, he was honored as Orangeburg's Citizen of the Year for his many years of community involvement.

Mr. Walsh was very active at Limestone Methodist Church, where he served as a Sunday school teacher, the church lay leader and chairman of both the administrative board and the finance committee.

He married the former Hessie Doyle Culler, and they had three children: Martha W. Lackey, James F. Walsh Jr. and Gary W. Walsh. He died in 2003 after a lifetime of community involvement.

Dr. T. Elliott Wannamaker (1909–1987)

T. Elliott Wannamaker was a highly esteemed industrialist, as well as an educator and a conservationist. As a chemical engineer, he founded the Wannamaker Chemical Company, which has evolved into Albemarle Corporation's Orangeburg plant.

Courtesy Braxton Wannamaker.

Elliott Wannamaker was born in Orangeburg in 1909 to William W. and Lyall M. Wannamaker. He was a graduate of Orangeburg High School in 1926 and received a degree in chemistry from The Citadel in 1930. In 1935, he was awarded a PhD in chemical engineering from Cornell University in New York.

From 1935 to 1937, Dr. Wannamaker was employed by Eastman Kodak in Rochester, New York. Wanting to start his own chemical business, he returned to Orangeburg in 1937 to establish the Wannamaker

Chemical Company. Initially, it manufactured dyes for the fur industry. Soon afterward, it began to be involved in the production of explosives. When World War II came about, he developed a procedure for producing tetryl, which was used as a primer for explosives. For its outstanding service to the war effort, Wannamaker Chemical Company received the army-navy E-citation. Dr. Wannamaker himself served in the United States Army Ordnance Corps.

After World War II, the company continued to produce tetryl and also became a leader in the production of gasoline additives. In 1953, Dr. Wannamaker sold the plant to the Ethyl Corporation but continued to serve as a consultant. Later, he formed a chemical development company and also was a consultant in the chemical industry.

In 1964, he became involved in the formation of Wade Hampton Academy, an Orangeburg prep school. Later, he founded Willington Academy and served as president of the South Carolina Independent School Association as well.

Dr. Wannamaker was a member of the advisory boards to Clemson University and Limestone College. He was a member of the American Chemical Society and served on the board of Minerals and Chemical Corporation. Additionally, he served on the board of the Epilepsy Association of South Carolina.

Elliott Wannamaker was widely known for his efforts to build ponds in the countryside.

He married the former Angie Ray Bryant, and they had four children: Thomas E. Wannamaker Jr., twins Robert B. and Lyall M. Wannamaker and Dr. Braxton B. Wannamaker. Dr. Wannamaker died in 1987.

DR. CLEMMIE E. WEBBER (B. 1913)

Dr. Clemmie Webber's boundless energy has been a blessing to the citizens of Orangeburg. Her contributions to humanity are endless. Being named both South Carolina Mother of the Year and National Mother of the Year only exemplifies the true character of such a rare jewel.

Clemmie Embly Webber was born in 1913 in St. Matthews to Henry W. and Colin Embly. At age three, she and her family moved to Orangeburg. She received her early education at the elementary department at Claflin University and her high school education at what is now South Carolina State University. In 1935, she graduated with a BS degree in chemistry at

Courtesy Paul Webber III.

SC State as well as received a master's there in 1952. Her doctorate degree was earned at American University in 1966. She has pursued further graduate study as well. Clemmie Webber has been involved in education throughout her entire career. She has taught at the elementary and high school levels, as well as being a professor at SC State for twenty-five years.

For almost twenty years, Dr. Webber and her husband operated two progressive businesses in Orangeburg, the College Soda Shop and the Riverside Soda Shop. Through these businesses, they provided practical experiences in life for college students by providing them with jobs to work their way through school. They genuinely nurtured and cared for many young people trying to further themselves in life.

Dr. Webber has been active in many youth-oriented areas. Among these were Cub Scout den mother, the Jack and Jill program, PTA president at two schools, the Sunlight Club and the Girl Scout program.

Her interest in quality education continued as she served on the Orangeburg School District 5 Board of Trustees from 1970 to 1981, being the chairman for six of those years. Additionally, she has served as president of the South Carolina School Boards Association.

Dr. Webber served on the Orangeburg Human Relations Council to help secure mutual understanding and cooperation between the races. In 1983, she was chosen not only as South Carolina's Mother of the Year but also the impressive honor of National Mother of the Year for the entire United States. She was selected as Orangeburg's Citizen of the Year in 2003 for her outstanding service through the years. In 2008, one of Orangeburg's city streets was renamed Webber Boulevard in honor of her and her husband's many endeavors to benefit Orangeburg.

At age eighty-nine, Clemmie Webber authored her first book, which was about her childhood neighborhood on Treadwell Street. This was followed at age ninety-two by her second book, about her College Soda Shop experiences.

In 1935, she married Paul R. Webber Jr., and they had three children: Judge Paul R. Webber III, Dr. Carolyn W. Thomson and Sheryl W. Washington. Dr. Clemmie Webber has truly exemplified excellence through her civic deeds, her educational endeavors and her values through the years.

PAUL R. WEBBER JR. (1911–1991)

In an editorial in *The Times and Democrat*, Paul R. Webber Jr. was referred to as the "Santa of the Century" for his deep caring and concerns for the young people of Orangeburg. He was a perfect example of practicing the Golden Rule.

Courtesy Paul Webber III.

Paul Webber Jr. was born in Gadsden, South Carolina, in 1911 to Paul R. Webber Sr. and Carrie A. Webber. His high school education was obtained at Booker T. Washington High School in Columbia, and he graduated from what is now South Carolina State University in 1933. Later, he received a master's degree in economics from Columbia University.

Early in his career, Mr. Webber served as a junior high principal and a farm demonstration agent. In 1938, he joined the faculty at South Carolina State University, where he taught economics for twenty-two years. He and his wife, Clemmie Webber, owned and operated the College Soda Shop and the Riverside Soda Shop. Many college students helped earn their way through school by working there, not to mention learning valuable experiences in life. One of these students ultimately became the chief justice of the South Carolina Supreme Court.

After his tenure teaching at South Carolina State University, he was an economic specialist for the State of South Carolina for seventeen years. Being involved in many business enterprises, he also owned Webber Motor Sales and Webber Housing.

Athletics played a major role in Paul Webber's life. He was an assistant football coach at his alma mater, where he earned All Southern honors as an end on its football team when he was a student athlete. Baseball also was dear to his heart, as he founded and coached the Orangeburg Tigers, a semipro team in the 1940s and 1950s.

Paul Webber and his wife were vitally concerned about the youth in the community. They taught young men and women valuable lessons in life through many wholesome social activities they sponsored, as well as many youth-oriented neighborhood athletic activities.

Mr. Webber belonged to many professional and civic organizations. Among them were the Guardsmen, Shriners, Masons and the Alpha Phi Alpha Fraternity. At Mount Pisgah Baptist Church, he served on the trustee board for many years.

Paul Webber married the former Clemmie Embly, and they had three children: Judge Paul Webber III, Dr. Carolyn W. Thomson and Sheryl W. Washington. He died in 1991 after a lifetime of providing meaningful experiences in the lives of young people in Orangeburg.

Elizabeth D. Whetsell (1912–1989)

Mrs. Elizabeth Whetsell was a prominent civic and cultural leader in Orangeburg for many years.

Elizabeth Whetsell was born in Spartanburg to Thomas H. and Bessie B. Daniel. She grew up there and in Washington, D.C. She graduated from Converse College in 1933 and furthered her education at Columbia University. Upon her marriage to Dr. William O. Whetsell in 1938, she moved to Orangeburg.

As a civic and cultural leader in the state, she expended much energy bringing musical and cultural events to Orangeburg. Mrs. Whetsell was one

Courtesy Bill Whetsell Jr.

of the founders and leaders of the Orangeburg Community Concert Series. For the last twenty years of her life, she reviewed books for a number of publishing companies throughout the Southeast and the East Coast. Many of these reviews were published in Orangeburg's local newspaper, *The Times and Democrat*, where she also wrote a weekly column entitled "Entertainment and the Arts."

Elizabeth Whetsell was an active participant in many community organizations. Among these were the Orangeburg Music Club, the Dogwood Garden Club and the Daughters of the American Revolution. She was also a founding member of both the Tuesday Book Club and the Friends of the Library. She served as president of the Auxiliary of the South Carolina Medical Association.

Religiously, Mrs. Whetsell was very active at St. Paul's Methodist Church, where she served on the Administrative Board, the Council on Ministries and as chairman of the music committee. She played the piano at services on many occasions, as well as served as an interim organist. She was a vital part of St. Paul's music program throughout her entire adult life there.

In 1938, she married Dr. William O. Whetsell, himself a prominent Orangeburg physician and community leader. They had two sons: Dr. William O. Whetsell Jr. and T. Daniel Whetsell. She died in 1989 after playing a major role in the cultural activities of Orangeburg for many years.

M. Heyward Whetsell (1906–1992)

Heyward Whetsell was a leader in the banking industry in Orangeburg. He was also at the forefront of forestry in South Carolina.

Mr. Whetsell was born near Bowman in 1906 to Wade Hampton and Pansy Hutto Whetsell. He grew up on a farm near Bowman and attended a one-room school until college. He attended Clemson College and graduated from the University of South Carolina in 1927 with a degree in business administration.

Courtesy Elsie Stevens.

His first employment was as a bookkeeper and later assistant vice-president at the Southern Bank and Trust Co. in Orangeburg. This bank closed during the Depression, so he then organized the Orangeburg Cash Depository with Harry Smoak and Henry Sims. In 1934, the Southern National Bank was organized, and he became the cashier there. In 1948, he became the president, a position he held for many years. In 1969, this bank merged with State Bank and Trust Co. and then became known as Bankers Trust. He continued to lead the Orangeburg offices until his retirement.

In addition to his banking career, Mr. Whetsell was a timber farmer and very active in various forestry organizations in South Carolina. He served on the Orangeburg County Forestry Board and was chairman of the State Advisory Committee of County Forestry Boards.

Heyward Whetsell spent much time and energy toward the well-being of the community. He was president of the Orangeburg County Tuberculosis Association, county chairman of the war bond drive in World War II, an officer of the Chamber of Commerce and president of the Lions Club. He was chairman of the first United Fund campaign for Orangeburg County and a leader in that organization for many years.

Mr. Whetsell was president of the South Carolina Bankers Association and a director of the South Carolina Chamber of Commerce. He also served on the Orangeburg Calhoun Technical College Foundation Board.

At St. Paul's Methodist Church, he was chairman of the Administrative Board and was the church treasurer for many years.

He married the former Elsie Rice, and they had two children: Elsie W. Stevens and Heyward Whetsell Jr. He died in 1992 after a long and distinguished career in the banking, forestry and civic arenas.

DR. WILLIAM O. WHETSELL (1912–1995)

As a physician for fifty years, Dr. William O. Whetsell was known for his compassionate caring for his patients. As the first medical director of the Methodist Home for the Aging, he served the healthcare needs of the elderly there for thirty-three years.

Dr. Bill Whetsell was born near Bowman in 1912 to Wade Hampton and Pansy Hutto Whetsell. He graduated from Wofford College in 1933 and the Medical College of South Carolina in 1937. After an internship at Columbia Hospital, he opened his practice in Orangeburg in 1938.

Courtesy Bill Whetsell Jr.

Dr. Whetsell served as chief of staff at the Orangeburg Regional Hospital on two occasions. He also served on the South Carolina Board of Medical Examiners for sixteen years, as well as being its president from 1973 to 1975. He was a charter member and past president of the South Carolina Academy of Family Practice. Dr. Whetsell also served as president of the Alumni Association at the Medical University of South Carolina. Serving as the medical director of the Methodist Home was a special passion for him in being able to provide for the healthcare needs of the elderly.

Civically, Dr. Whetsell led a full and active life. He was a member of the board of trustees for both the Orangeburg City Schools and the Orangeburg County Board of Education. He was very active with the Boy Scouts and was a longtime member of the Lions Club. Dr. Whetsell also served on the board of visitors at Columbia College, the board of trustees at Spartanburg Junior College and the Committee of One Hundred at Emory University. Additionally, he was on the board of trustees at Orangeburg Regional Hospital.

Dr. Whetsell was listed in *Marquis' Who's Who in the Southeast* in 1965 and *Personalities of the South* in 1979. In 1983, he was selected as the Citizen of the Year in Orangeburg for his many endeavors to benefit the city and its citizens.

He retired after fifty years of service as a physician. Among Dr. Whetsell's hobbies were camellia gardening and being an avid outdoorsman. He was an active member at St. Paul's Methodist Church.

Upon his graduation from medical school, he married the former Elizabeth Daniel, and they had two sons: Dr. William O. Whetsell Jr. and T. Daniel Whetsell. After a compassionate career of tending to the healthcare needs of Orangeburg, Dr. Whetsell died in 1995.

JUDGE KAREN J. WILLIAMS (B. 1951)

Judge Karen J. Williams has served with honor and distinction as a federal judge for the Fourth Circuit of the United States Court of Appeals. In 1992, she became that court's first female member and, in 2007, became its first female chief judge.

Judge Williams was born in Orangeburg County in 1951 to Dr. James G. Johnson and Mrs. Marcia R. Johnson (later Dantzler). After receiving her elementary and high school education in Orangeburg, she graduated from Columbia College in 1972. She taught English and social studies for several years afterward. In 1980, she graduated cum laude from the University of South Carolina's School of Law. Mrs. Williams was admitted to the bar and practiced with her husband and father-in-law's firm from 1980 to 1992. In 1992, she was appointed by the president to serve on the Fourth Circuit of the United States Court of Appeals, which was headquartered in Richmond, Virginia. Judge Williams was appointed chief judge of the Fourth Circuit in 2007 and served in that capacity until her retirement in 2009.

She holds memberships in many professional associations. Her civic endeavors include the Rotary Club, the Business and Professional Women's Club and the Junior Service League. Judge Williams has also served on the University of South Carolina School of Law Advisory Board, the board of directors of the Regional Medical Center Foundation, the board of visitors of Columbia College, the Orangeburg-Calhoun Technical College Advisory Board, the board of directors of the National Judicial Center and the board of trustees for Woodberry Forest School.

Courtesy Karen Williams.

Judge Williams has received many awards and honors throughout her career. Among these are an honorary doctor of laws from Claflin University in 1991, an honorary doctorate of English from Columbia College in 1995, an honorary doctor of laws from the University of South Carolina in 2009, the Distinguished Service Award from South Carolina State University in 1993, the Junior Service League Career Woman of the Year in 1979, 1981 and 1982, the Woman of Achievement Award from the Miss South Carolina pageant in 1994 and the Jean Galloway Bissell Award from the South Carolina Women Lawyers Association in 2007.

At First Baptist Church, she has served on numerous committees through the years as well as chairman of the trustees. She has been chosen as the commencement speaker at several high schools as well as at her alma mater, Columbia College and the University of South Carolina.

Judge Williams married Charles H. Williams II, and they have four children, all of whom finished law school. They are Marian W. Scalise, Ashley W. Groot, Charles H. Williams III and David Williams.

MARGARET S. WILLIAMS (B. 1920)

Margaret Williams has been considered one of Orangeburg's finest ambassadors and has been recognized for her many deeds of outstanding community service.

Margaret Shecut Williams was born in Orangeburg in 1920 to Marion A. and Winnie W. Shecut. She graduated from Orangeburg High School in 1937. Her family did not have the funds to be able to send her to college, but upon the recommendation of many people from Orangeburg, she received a dining room scholarship to attend Winthrop College. This allowed her to work her way through college, and she was able to graduate there in 1941. After college, she taught school for one year before her marriage in 1942.

Mrs. Williams has dedicated her life to the service of others. In 1946, she was one of the founders of the Junior Charity League, now known as the Junior Service League of Orangeburg. She served as the first president of this benevolent organization, which provides funds for many charitable projects to benefit Orangeburg. One of her dear ongoing projects through the years has been to beautify Orangeburg. Inspired by the noted cherry blossoms in Washington, she led the efforts in the early 1990s to enhance

Courtesy Charles Williams.

Orangeburg with many cherry tree plantings in Edisto Memorial Gardens and throughout the city streets. Through her husband, Senator Marshall B. Williams, state grants were obtained to assist in this project in addition to the local fundraising efforts. The Junior Service League also helped by selling cherry trees to individuals to plant in their yards at home. Additionally, Mrs. Williams has helped initiate storefront cleanup and painting projects in downtown Orangeburg.

Margaret Williams is especially proud of being able to encourage young people to go to college. She was able to assist many local students with jobs as pages through her husband in the South Carolina legislature in Columbia.

Mrs. Williams loves people and is known for her warm, outgoing personality. There are no strangers in her life. Sartorially, she loves hats and is rarely seen without a beautiful hat coordinated with her outfit.

For her many endeavors, Margaret Williams has been awarded the Order of the Palmetto, South Carolina's highest honor, as well as the Edisto Award from Orangeburg City Council.

In 1942, she married Marshall B. Williams. He went on to become the nation's longest-serving state senator. They had four children: M. Burns Williams Jr., Ann W. Platz, Mary Ashley W. Gardner and Charles H. Williams II. Mrs. Williams will always be known for her community pride and devotion to Orangeburg.

Senator Marshall B. Williams (1912–1995)

Senator Marshall B. Williams was Orangeburg's legendary senator for forty-three years. He also enjoyed the reputation as one of South Carolina's most outstanding trial lawyers.

Marshall Williams was born in 1912 near Norway, South Carolina, to Charles H. and Maude M. Williams. At age eleven, he moved to Orangeburg, where he remained for the rest of his life. He graduated from Orangeburg High School in 1929, the University of South Carolina in 1933 and the USC School of Law in 1936. After being admitted to the bar, he returned to Orangeburg and joined the law firm of Senator Henry Sims.

When World War II intervened, Mr. Williams volunteered for the navy and served as a gunnery and ordnance officer in the Pacific Theatre. He attained the rank of lieutenant commander during his service.

Upon his return from the war, Mr. Williams resumed the practice of law and was elected to South Carolina's House of Representatives in 1946,

Courtesy Charles Williams.

where he served for six years. In 1952, he was elected as Orangeburg's senator and served for forty-three years until his death. At the time, he was the longest-serving state senator in the United States.

While in the Senate, he was known for his low-key style, preferring to promote legislation behind the scenes instead of on the floor. He served on the Judiciary Committee from day one, an assignment rarely given to a freshman senator. In 1984, he became the chairman and guided the restructuring of state government, helped overhaul the state's ethics code, revised the Uniform Commercial Code and oversaw efforts to reform the state's civil justice system. In 1989, he was elected president pro tempore of the Senate. Senator Williams was a mover and a shaker in guiding legislation.

He was very active in civic and fraternal matters in Orangeburg. He was a member of the Elks, Shriners, Masons, Kiwanis Club, VFW and American Legion. Senator Williams was instrumental in the establishment of the Orangeburg-Calhoun Technical College, a leader in industrial recruitment for Orangeburg and a strong supporter for South Carolina State University in the legislature. He was known for his trademark bow ties and ever-present cigar that he chewed but never smoked.

Marshall Williams married the former Margaret Shecut, and they had four children: M. Burns Williams Jr., Ann W. Platz, Mary Ashley W. Gardner and Charles H. Williams II.

Senator Williams died in 1995 after a lifetime of service to his county and state.

Mary W. Williams (1916–2009)

Mrs. Mary Williams was probably the most tireless advocate for humanitarian deeds that Orangeburg has ever experienced. She was at the forefront of practically every endeavor to make Orangeburg a better place in which to live.

Mary Wright Williams was born in Shelton, South Carolina, to William E. and Edith C. Wright. She graduated from Winthrop College in 1937 after majoring in home economics. She then taught home economics at Orangeburg High School for two years and met her future husband while doing so.

Mrs. Williams has always been ahead of her time with humanitarian endeavors. She was a founding member of the Junior Service League in 1946, helped organize the United Way in Orangeburg in 1950, helped found the Orangeburg Girls' Attention Home in 1969 for girls in trouble, helped establish the American Field Service foreign exchange student program in Orangeburg in 1960 and personally hosted the first student in the program. Additionally, Mrs. Williams played an active role in organizing the Guardian Ad Litem program in Orangeburg in 1982, was a founding member of the Orangeburg Regional Hospital Auxiliary for volunteers in 1970 and established a mentoring program in the public schools in the 1980s. In the 1960s, she was a founding member and leader of the Orangeburg Human Relations Council to develop better human relations during the integration

Courtesy Mary Williams.

transition as well as after a racial incident involving deaths at South Carolina State University in 1968.

Mrs. Williams served on the boards of many benevolent organizations. Among these were the Lowcountry Council of Girl Scouts, the Florence Crittenden Home for Unwed Mothers in Charleston, the Head Start Advisory Board, the Office of Economic Opportunity board, the Orangeburg Area Rehabilitation Center board, the South Carolina Presbyterian Homes board, the Orangeburg-Calhoun Detention Center Board and the Downtown Orangeburg Revitalization Association board. She has also been heavily involved in Project Hope, an organization to promote a spirit of mutual cooperation among the races in Orangeburg.

Mary Williams has been the recipient of numerous awards for her humanitarian spirit and participation. Among these are the 1979 Citizen of the Year for Orangeburg, the 1983 Sertoma Club Service to Mankind Award, the Winthrop College Mary Mildred Sullivan Award, the Edisto Award for outstanding service to Orangeburg and the Order of the Palmetto in 2000, which is the highest award given by the State of South Carolina.

At First Presbyterian Church, she continued her leadership roles in being an elder, choir member and leader in the nursery department, youth department and with the young adults.

Mrs. Williams married R. Sumter Williams Jr., and they had two daughters: Vicki W. Culler and Carolyn W. Bricklemyer. She died in 2009 after a lifetime of service to Orangeburg. Her boundless energy to make Orangeburg a better place in which to live has literally touched the lives of thousands of people.

R. SUMTER WILLIAMS JR. (1915–1997)

Sumter Williams was a dedicated public servant in Orangeburg. The humanitarian role he and his wife, Mary Williams, played greatly enhanced Orangeburg through the years.

"Sump" Williams was born in Orangeburg in 1915 to Robert Sumter and Carolyn Salley Williams. He graduated from Orangeburg High School and the Darlington Academy in Georgia.

During World War II, Mr. Williams served in the Navy Seals in the Pacific Theatre. Upon his return in 1945, he was a salesman for McKesson, Robbins, & Co., a wholesale drug firm. He was decorated with the Philippines Liberation Medal, the World War II Victory Medal and the Asia-Pacific

Courtesy Mary Williams.

Campaign Medal. In 1950, he joined his father in business at Orangeburg Pharmacy, where he remained until his retirement.

Mr. Williams was very involved in civic affairs in Orangeburg. He was a member of the Human Relations Council, which was formed to establish mutual understanding and cooperation between the races during the years of racial turmoil in the 1960s and 1970s. He served on the original board of directors of the United Way for Orangeburg. From 1959 to 1972, Mr. Williams guided the local public schools as a member of the Orangeburg School District 5 Board of Trustees. In 1975, he was a gubernatorial appointment to the Orangeburg, Calhoun, Bamberg Alcohol and Drug Abuse Commission and served in that capacity for many years. He also served on the local board of Bankers Trust.

At First Presbyterian Church, Mr. Williams was a deacon, an elder and chairman of several scholarship funds. As a longtime member of the Rotary Club, he was named a Paul Harris Fellow.

Sumter Williams married the former Mary Wright, and they had two daughters: Vicki W. Culler and Carolyn W. Bricklemyer. He died in 1997.

F. HALL YARBOROUGH (1921–2004)

F. Hall Yarborough was a champion of fiscal responsibility in state government. He was the architect for the creation of the Legislative Audit Council, which monitors South Carolina's governmental spending.

Hall Yarborough was born in Jenkinsville to David Glenn Yarborough and Helen Whatley Yarborough in 1921. He graduated from the University of South Carolina in 1941 and was accepted to go into medical school, but World War II intervened. At that time, he enlisted in the Army Air Corps. Until being called to active duty, he filled in as a school principal in Wagener and met his future wife, who was teaching there. Once in the Air Corps,

Courtesy Elizabeth Yarborough.

he served as a navigator in the Air Transport Command. After the war, he and his wife settled in Orangeburg and pursued farming. Due to the lack of profitability in agriculture, he then became principal at Cameron High School. After that, he became the probation officer in Orangeburg under Judge Frank Haigler. During that time, he became interested in the legal profession and borrowed law books to follow the prescribed course of reading law. After successfully passing the bar exam, he was admitted to the bar in 1952 and practiced law in Orangeburg until shortly before his death at age eighty-two.

In 1956, Mr. Yarborough was elected to the South Carolina House of Representatives, where he served until 1974. He was one of the most respected legislators of his time. The creation of the Legislative Audit Council to "see that South Carolina's taxpayers' money goes to where it is supposed to go" was his passion for years. After stepping down from the legislature in 1974, he was the logical choice to be on the Audit Council and served as its chairman for ten years.

Mr. Yarborough was a commissioner with the Soil Conservation Service for thirty years and was a director of the Edisto Farm Credit Service for twenty years. He was appointed chairman for Orangeburg County's Bicentennial Committee to coordinate our nation's 200th anniversary celebration in 1976.

For his service to South Carolina, Mr. Yarborough was awarded the state's highest honor, the Order of the Palmetto, in 1988. For his service to Orangeburg, he was selected as the 1996 Citizen of the Year.

Hall Yarborough was a member of the Lions Club and the Rotary Club in Orangeburg. At First Baptist Church, he served as a deacon as well as a Sunday school teacher.

Mr. Yarborough married the former Elizabeth Wolfe, and they had four children: Foster, Tom, Beth and Bill. He died in 2004 after a distinguished career serving South Carolina.

Geraldyne P. Zimmerman (b. 1911)

Mrs. Gerry Zimmerman has probably been one of the most prolific civic leaders Orangeburg has known. Her untiring efforts guiding the lives of children and young women are unparalleled.

Born in 1911 in Orangeburg to James Arthur Pierce and Hazel Tatnall Pierce, she has lived her entire life in the Orangeburg community. Her elementary education was obtained at Claflin College and high school at

Courtesy Gerry Zimmerman.

what is now South Carolina State University. Collegiately, she graduated from Fisk University in Nashville, Tennessee, in 1932 and received a master's degree in mathematics from South Carolina State University. She did further study at Pennsylvania State University, Rutgers University, San Jose State College and Carlton College. As a math teacher at South Carolina State University for thirty-one years, Mrs. Zimmerman wrote several papers and handbooks regarding academics. Additionally, she wrote and produced three Educational Television (ETV) tapes for the South Carolina Department of Education in 1961.

"Mrs. Z," as she has been affectionately called, was a dynamo in community affairs. As a leader in the Girl Scouts for over fifty years, she has served as a troop leader, board member, association president, troop consultant and service unit chairman. For her untiring efforts, she was awarded its highest honor, the Thanks-Badge. As a neighborhood organizer with the Peasley Street Playground, the community center building built there was named the Zimmerman Community Center for her outstanding leadership and guidance through the years. She has been a leader in the

Sunlight Club to provide wholesome activities as well as instill character for the youth of Orangeburg. In 1963, she organized the Helen Sheffield Girls' Club, a federated community service club for girls, and helped guide its success for many years.

Through her efforts and coordination, the historic old African American cemetery in Orangeburg was cleaned up from a dilapidated state and revitalized into a place of dignity. She was instrumental in raising the funds to do so as well as securing the City of Orangeburg to maintain this historic cemetery, known as the Orangeburg Cemetery.

Mrs. Zimmerman also was the co-organizer of Links, Inc. as a local civic club. She has been active with the Orangeburg City Beautification Advisory Council, the Orangeburg County Association for Retarded Citizens and the Ethyl Corporation Community Advisory Panel and has served as the Red Cross Board chairman and past president of the Orangeburg County Literacy Association. She also was a volunteer for both the United Way and the Salvation Army and served on the Cooperative Church Ministries of Orangeburg board, which provides clothing and food for the local indigent population. She has been a very active member at St. Paul's Episcopal Church.

For her outstanding efforts in making Orangeburg a better place in which to live, Mrs. Zimmerman was selected as Orangeburg's Citizen of the Year in 1994. In 2000, she was awarded South Carolina's highest award for community service, the Order of the Palmetto. South Carolina State University awarded her its Humanitarian and Education Council Award in 2003, and later that same year, she was selected for the South Carolina Black Hall of Fame. She received the Distinguished Alumni Award from SC State, and in 1999 the City of Orangeburg bestowed her with its highest award for community service, the Edisto Award.

Gerry Zimmerman married Dudley M. Zimmerman, and they had two children: D. Malone Zimmerman Jr. and Rose Hayzel Z. Jones. Mrs. Zimmerman is considered to be one of the finest humanitarians Orangeburg has known.

INDEX

A

Ackerman, Hugo 95
Albergotti, James M. 31
Amick, H. Ciremba 96
Atkinson, W. Eugene 32

B

Bennett, Leonard 34
Berry, J. Andrew, Jr. 98
Berry, Joseph A. 35
Berry, Willie 99
Bethea, Wallace C. 36
Bowman, Judge Ilderton Wesley 38
Brailsford, James M. 39
Brailsford, Judge James M., Jr. 100
Brantley, Thomas F. 40
Brewington, A.L. "Red" 102
Brown, Alec T. 103
Bryant, Thomas B., Jr. 105
Bull, Norman A. 9
Bythewood, Alton E. 42
Bythewood, Thaddeus K., Sr. 106

C

Cauthen, James C. 43
Cheatham, Martin C., Jr. 107
Clark, William J. 108
Cleckley, J. Fischer 44
Cornelson, George H. 10
Covington, Jane C. 110
Cox, William B., Sr. 111
Cunningham, Austin 113

D

Dash, Laval David 45
Davis, Reverend George E. 46
Dawson, Oliver C. 47
Dean, Julian Hubert 114
Dibble, Andrew 49
Dibble, Samuel 12
Dibble, T.O.S. 50
Dukes, Earl 115
Dukes, John H. 13
Dukes, J.W.H. 14
Dukes, W. Hampton 51
Dukes, William R. 117
Dukes, William W., Jr. 118
Dunton, Reverend Lewis M. 15

E

Elliott, Dr. Thomas A. 16

F

Fair, S. Clyde 120
Fischer, Clarence A., Sr. 121
Fischer, G. Herman 52
Fogle, Samuel T. 122
Fordham, Florella 53
Fordham, John Hammond 17
Frampton, Reverend W. McLeod, Jr. 124
Furchgott, Dr. Robert F. 125

G

Garick, Lawrence T., Sr. 127
Glaze, William L. 18
Glover, Judge Thomas W. 19
Gramling, Betty Lane 128

H

Herbert, Daniel O. 54
Hoffmeyer, Reverend J.F.M. 130
Horger, Charlton B. 131
Horne, Jesse E. "Dick" 132
Howard, Robert E. 134
Hudson, Edward O. 136
Hughes, Judge Jerry M. 55
Hunt, James B., Jr. 137

I

Izlar, Judge James F. 20

J

Jarvis Brothers 138
Jeffries, Willie 140
Jennings, Octavia M. 56
Jennings, Robert H., Jr. 59
Jennings, Robert H., Sr. 57
Johnstone, Alan McC. 141

K

Kohn, Theodore 21

L

Lide, Robert 60
Limehouse, Frank F., Jr. 143
Livingston, Dean B. 145
Livingston, Mason 146
Livingston, William A. 61
Louis, Deopold 23
Lusty, Arthur J., Jr. 148
Lusty, Lois D. 148

M

Mabry, H. Filmore 149
Manning, Dr. Hubert V. 151
Marchant, Daniel H. 63
Marshall, Harris A., Sr. 152
Maxwell, John M. 64
McLafferty, Dee H. 153
McLees, Reverend James L. 65
McLeod, Harold M., Sr. 155
McTeer, Dr. E. Benjamin 67
Mellichamp, Stiles R. 24
Middleton, Earl M. 156
Mikels, Roy 158
Miller, Thomas E. 25
Mirmow, Edward V. 68
Mobley, Dr. Charles A. 69
Moss, Judge B. Hart 70
Mutch, Mildred "Skip" 159

N

Nance, Dr. M. Maceo, Jr. 161
Newton, R. Park 162
Nix, Reverend Nelson C. 71

O

Osborne, Rutledge L. 163

P

Pace, Captain James C. 165
Pearson, John F. 72
Pendarvis, Edward O., Sr. 166

R

Rheney, Joyce W. 167
Riggs, Harpin 26
Riggs, Walter M. 74
Roquemore, James W. 169
Rosen, Judge Louis 170
Runager, Gerald E. 172
Rushton, Dr. Edward W. 173

S

Salley, Alexander S. 75
Salley, Dr. Alexander S. 27
Salley, Dr. Raymond R. 77
Salley, Marion 76
Salley, T. Elliott 78
Sheffield, Helen W. 175
Sheridan, Hugo G. 28
Sheriff, Dr. Hilla 176
Sims, Henry R. 79
Sims, Hugo S., Jr. 177
Sims, Hugo S., Sr. 80
Sims, Lucile H. 179
Smith, W. Eugene 180
Smoak, J.W. 82
Smoak, Perry M. 83
Staley, Frank M., Jr. 182
Sulton, James E. 183
Summers, Anabel 184
Summers, Judge Carroll 186
Summers, J. West, Sr. 84
Summers, Thomas S. 187

T

Thackston, Albert J. 85
Thackston, Dr. Lawrence P., Sr. 86
Tisdale, Dr. Henry N. 188
Tourville, Frank P., Sr. 190
Tribble, Bernice W. 191
Tyler, Lillie Mae 193

U

Ulmer, C. Frederic 194

W

Walsh, James F., Sr. 196
Wannamaker, Jacob G. 30
Wannamaker, Lilla S. 87
Wannamaker, T. Elliott 197
Wannamaker, William W. 88
Webber, Dr. Clemmie E. 198
Webber, Paul R., Jr. 200
Whetsell, Dr. William O. 204
Whetsell, Elizabeth D. 201
Whetsell, M. Heyward 203
Whittaker, Dr. Miller F. 89
Wilkinson, Dr. Robert S. 92
Wilkinson, Marion B. 91
Williams, Judge Karen J. 206
Williams, Margaret S. 208
Williams, Mary W. 211
Williams, R. Sumter, Jr. 212
Williams, Senator Marshall B. 209

Y

Yarborough, F. Hall 214

Z

Zimmerman, Geraldyne P. 215

ABOUT THE AUTHOR

Courtesy Gene Atkinson.

Dr. Gene Atkinson is an Orangeburg dentist and local historian. He has been recognized for his civic endeavors, his historical collections on Orangeburg and his contributions to dentistry.

Dr. Atkinson has authored two pictorial histories on Orangeburg and has served on numerous local committees and boards. He chaired the Stevenson Auditorium Renovation Committee and raised the funds to do this glorious revitalization. This grand old city venue won much acclaim after a five-year renovation, including the South Carolina Downtown Association's award for the best downtown building restoration in South Carolina in 2001.

In dentistry, he established South Carolina's national award-winning National Children's Dental Health Month programs. He has received mastership status in both the Academy of General Dentistry and the American Society of Dentistry for Children. Additionally, he was presented the Meritorious Achievement Award from the South Carolina Dental Association in 1996 and the American Society of Dentistry for Children in

1998. In 2004, Dr. Atkinson was named as Orangeburg's Citizen of the Year for his many contributions to Orangeburg life. He received the prestigious Order of the Palmetto award in 2010.

Dr. Atkinson also entertains residents of retirement homes, church groups and local organizations with informative slideshow presentations. He is an avid hiker and takes groups on expeditions to many of America's national parks.

Interesting and Influential People of Orangeburg will showcase Dr. Atkinson's work on some of the movers and shakers in Orangeburg's past who helped shape its destiny through the years.